THE USBORNE BOOK OF
EUROPE

Rebecca Treays

Designed by Paul Greenleaf and Rebecca Halverson

Illustrated by Nicholas Hewetson

Additional Illustrations by Mark Bergin and Jason Lewis
Map Illustrations by Jeremy Gower

Edited by Jane Chisholm
Series Designer: Amanda Barlow

Consultants: Dr. Christopher Smith
Martin Bond, Patricia Fara, Dr. Alison Henwood, Dr. Anne Millard,
Dr. Stelios Stavridis, Dr. Richard Vinen

CONTENTS

INTRODUCTION

WHAT IS EUROPE?

An 18th century Dutch map of Europe

Europe is one of the seven large areas of land, called continents, which make up the Earth. The other six are Asia, Australasia, Africa, North and South America and Antarctica.

Europe is an irregular shaped peninsula jutting out of Asia. Three of its frontiers are formed by indisputable physical features: the Atlantic Ocean in the west, the Mediterranean Sea in the south, and the Arctic Ocean in the north. In the east there is no obvious boundary, but traditionally geographers take the Ural Mountains and the River Ural as the eastern border of the continent. The southeast boundary follows the line of the Caucasian Mountains and the north coast of the Black Sea around to the Aegean Sea (see map, pages 4-5).

These geographical boundaries also correspond loosely with certain shared European influences, such as language (see page 12), Greek and Roman civilization (see pages 10-11, 14-16), Christianity (see page 18), political systems, alliances and conflicts.

Occasionally, historians use the term European more narrowly, to mean only those countries which were influenced by the western Christian Church in Rome, rather than those influenced by the eastern Christian Church in Constantinople (see page 18).

Today, particularly in the media, you will often hear the term Europe used to refer only to those countries which belong to the European Community (see page 40).

WHAT'S IN A NAME?

The word Europe first appears in the feminine form as the goddess Europa in Greek mythology. According to legend, Europa was the daughter of Agenor, king of Phoenicia. The god Zeus fell in love with her, and after having turned into a white bull, he abducted her. They swam westward from the shore of Asia Minor (now Turkey) and landed on the Greek island of Crete. But this does not seem reason enough to give her name to the whole continent.

As a geographical term, the name Europe first appears in a Greek poem from the 8th century BC. But it applied only to northern mainland Greece. The Ancient Greek historian, Herodotus, was the first to use the expression to describe a larger land mass. According to him, his compatriots divided the world into three parts: Europe, Asia and Libya (now called Africa). But he admitted that he did not know where the terms had originated. Modern historians are none the wiser.

Illustration from an Ancient Greek vase showing Europa being abducted by Zeus.

In Greek, the literal meaning of *europe* is "far-sighted", from the Greek word *eurus,* which means "broad", and *optikos,* which means "of the eye". But some people think that both the names Asia and Europe come from the ancient language of Akkadian which was spoken in Mesopotamia (present-day Iraq). In Akkadian *asu* means "rise" and *erebu* means "enter". *Asu*, giving the name Asia, refers to the east, where the sun rises. *Erebu*, giving the name Europe, refers to the west, where the sun sets.

DATES AND DEFINITIONS

Some of the dates in this book are from before the birth of Christ. They are followed by the letters BC (Before Christ). For example, 50BC means 50 years before Christ's birth. Dates after Christ's birth are sometimes preceded by the letters AD, which stand for *anno Domini* (The Year of Our Lord). Some dates begin with the abbreviation "c." This stands for *circa*, Latin for "about". It is used when historians are unsure exactly when an event took place.

The terms western and eastern Europe are used in the book to describe loose geographical areas. The terms Western and Eastern Europe (with capital letters) are used only when referring to the political areas either side of the Iron Curtain (see page 38).

The glossary defines many of the more complex words you will come across.

GEOGRAPHICAL EUROPE

From the Urals to the Atlantic Ocean, Europe covers 10,400,000km² (4,000,000 square miles) and makes up 8% of the Earth's surface.

Almost the entire eastern half of Europe is covered by a massive plain which stretches for 5,000,000km² (1,930,000 square miles), broken only in central Russia by a few relatively low hills.

In contrast, western Europe is a mosaic of different landscapes. In the south, mountain ranges with steep rugged sides and snowy peaks encircle the Mediterranean Sea. Below them lie flat green plains, such as the Po Valley in Italy and the Hungarian Plain. Much of north-western Europe is a gently changing pattern of valleys and rolling hills.

The northern mountains of Scandinavia and Scotland are less dramatic than those in the south because they are older. They have been worn down over millions of years by rain, wind and glaciers.

Europe has several large navigable rivers and an intricate coast line with many sheltered shores which are suitable for landing ships. This has shaped its history making Europe a continent of sailors, traders and explorers.

NORWEGIAN SEA

NORTH SEA

BRITISH ISLES

GRAMPIANS

Irish Sea

Severn

Thames

English Channel

ATLANTIC OCEAN

Seine

Rhine

Elbe

Loire

Rhône

MASSIF CENTRAL

Mt. Blanc ▲ ALPS

Po

APENNIN

Garonne

PYRENEES

Ebro

APENNIN

Tagus

Guadalquivir

MEDITERR

AFRICA

SIBERIA

ASIA

URAL MOUNTAINS

Pechora

Severnaya Dvina

DINAVIA

Ladoga

NORTH EUROPEAN PLAIN

Volga

Dvina

Baltic Sea

Countries to the east of the Baltic
Sea are often called the Baltic states.

Vistula

Neisse

Ural

Volga

CARPATHIANS

Dnieper

Dniester

Don

UNGARIAN PLAIN

Danube

Tisza

Danube

CAUCASUS

Mt. Elbrus

INARIC ALPS

BALKAN MOUNTAINS

BLACK SEA

riatic Sea

The Balkan Mountains give their
name to the Balkans, the region
between the Aegean Sea and
southern Hungarian Plain.

Dardenelles

ASIA MINOR

Aegean
Sea

EUROPEAN RECORD BREAKERS

Highest mountain - Mount Elbrus 5,633m
(18,481ft)

Biggest island - Great Britain 229,885km²
(88,764 square miles)

Biggest lake - Ladoga 18,400km²
(7,105 square miles)

Longest river - Volga 3,531km
(2,194 miles)

JEAN SEA

THE SHAPING OF EUROPE

Scientists believe that it took millions of years for Europe to become the shape it is today. They think that the surface of the Earth is divided into a series of plates, which fit together like a jigsaw puzzle.

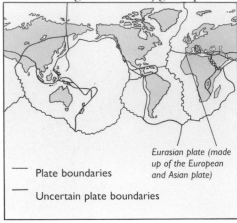

Eurasian plate (made up of the European and Asian plate)

— Plate boundaries

— Uncertain plate boundaries

Each plate is made up of something called continental crust (which forms land) and oceanic crust (which forms the oceans' floors). Plates are continually moving very slowly, at about the same rate as your fingernails grow. Scientists think that many of the features of Europe's landscape were caused by plate movements. As plates shift, the position of the oceans and continents on the Earth's surface changes. The maps below show how the continents have shifted over hundreds of millions of years. The arrangement of the present-day continent is shown in green.

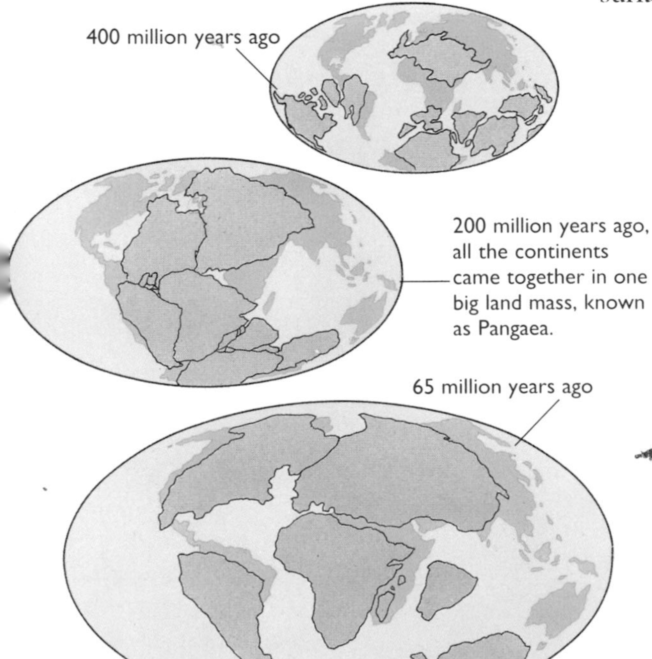

THE BEGINNINGS OF THE ATLANTIC OCEAN

The Atlantic Ocean began to open up about fifty million years ago, when the European plate and the North Atlantic plate started to drift apart. As the plates divided, a hot syrupy substance made of molten (melted) rock, called magma, was forced upward from below the crust. As the magma reached the Earth's surface, it hardened to form new oceanic crust. This process is still going on and the Atlantic Ocean is getting wider by as much as 4cm (1.5in) per year.

VOLCANOES

Volcanoes are holes in the Earth's crust out of which magma and gas have erupted. This happens whenever there is a big enough build up of magma and gas beneath their surface. There are over 80 active volcanoes in Europe, 62 of which are in Iceland. Around the southern tip of Italy there are four volcanoes: Etna, Stromboli, Vesuvius and Vulcano. These formed when oceanic crust on the African plate boundary was pushed underneath continental crust on the Eurasian plate (see diagram above). The oceanic crust melted and formed magma. The continental crust above, weakened by the collision, could not prevent the molten crust from bursting through the surface in a volcanic eruption.

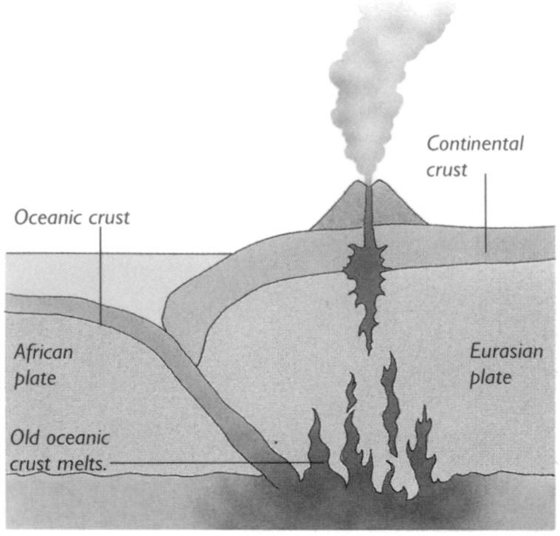

Oceanic crust

Continental crust

African plate

Eurasian plate

Old oceanic crust melts.

This diagram shows how volcanoes happen.

In December 1991, Mount Etna in Sicily, erupted for the 21st time since 1971. Lava spewed from the mountain at the rate of a million tonnes a day and poured down to the small village of Safferana. Luckily for the inhabitants, the lava flow slowed down enough to be diverted before it engulfed the village.

This picture shows farm cottages submerged by lava on the lower slopes of Mount Etna during the 1991 eruption.

As the burning lava poured down the mountain, everything in its path was destroyed.

The Italian flag

Graffiti on the side of this barn sarcastically thanks the government. In fact, many local people thought that it should have done more to help them.

GRAZIE GOVERNO

400 million years ago

200 million years ago, all the continents came together in one big land mass, known as Pangaea.

65 million years ago

MAKING MOUNTAIN RANGES

Mountain ranges are formed when plates push against each other. The Alps, Pyrenees, Sierra Nevada, Carpathian Mountains and Balkan Mountains all arose about 65 million years ago, when the Eurasian plate and the African plate were forced into each other. Mountains grew as flat rock layers buckled and sediment (particles of rock) which had collected on the sea floor was pushed up onto the land. Every year the Alps get a little higher. Scientists think that this is because the African and the Eurasian plate are still crunching into each other.

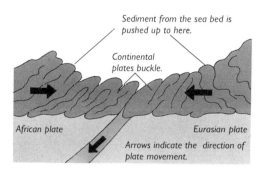

Sediment from the sea bed is pushed up to here.

Continental plates buckle.

African plate   Eurasian plate

Arrows indicate the direction of plate movement.

CRACKING PLATES

As plates move, cracks, called faults, appear in the Earth's crust. Chunks of crust between two faults can collapse to form valleys, or be pushed up into mountains, called block mountains. A valley between two block mountains is called a rift. The Rhine Valley in Germany is a rift, created by the mountains of the Vosges and the Black Forest.

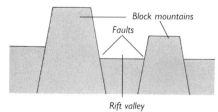

Block mountains

Faults

Rift valley

The Rhine Valley

THE ICE AGES

About two million years ago, the climate began to cool and a period of ice ages began. During each ice age, northern Europe was blanketed with moving sheets of ice, called glaciers, each as much as two kilometres (one and a half miles) thick. In southern Europe, only the mountain ranges were glaciated.

A present-day glacier in the Alps

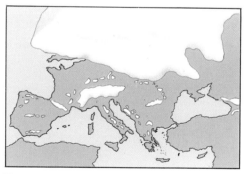

The extent of glaciation at the height of the last ice age

In between each ice age were warmer interglacial periods, when the temperature rose and, except in the very north and on mountains, the glaciers melted. There have probably been more than 20 separate cycles of glaciation and melting over the last two million years. At the moment we are in an interglacial period that started about 10,000 years ago. The European landscape carries the evidence of the glaciation/thawing process. Many valleys, especially in the north of Europe,

are glacial valleys. They were formed as glaciers moved, scraping out the rock below them. When the ice melted, u-shaped valleys were revealed. The fjords of Scandinavia are glacial valleys that flooded when sea levels rose as the ice melted at the end of the last ice age.

The rock and sediment which is dislodged and carried by the moving glaciers is called moraine. As the glaciers moved south, they melted and deposited moraine. Over thousands of years, this built up to form flat plains. The great plains of eastern Europe are made of moraine.

A Norwegian fjord

THE FIRST EUROPEANS

A woolly bison - food for the first settlers

Early people, known as *Homo erectus,* first lived in Europe about 730,000 years ago. But *Homo sapiens,* from whom modern humans are descended, did not set foot on the continent until nearly 700,000 years later. Many scientists believe that *Homo sapiens* evolved in Africa about 300,000 years ago, but only arrived in Europe during the last ice age around 30,000BC. These people, who can be called the first Europeans, probably came in search of food, following herds of migrating bison, reindeer and mammoths. They would have crossed into Europe via the Dardenelles. This is now a stretch of water separating Turkey and Greece, but in those days it was a landbridge.

As the ice age came to an end, ice sheets retreated toward the North Pole and plant and animal life began to flourish. *Homo sapiens* moved slowly northward into the new fertile plains of Europe.

THE STONE AGE

Archeologists group early people into periods according to what their tools were made of. As the earliest evidence of *Homo sapiens* in Europe consists of stone and bone tools, the people who used them are said to belong to the Stone Age. The Stone Age is divided into three stages: the Palaeolithic (old), the Mesolithic (middle) and the Neolithic (new). These stages are not given precise dates, because they occurred at different times in different places. But most experts think that all of Europe had entered the Neolithic Age by 4000BC.

The first Europeans probably lived together in groups of about 25 to 30, in caves or rough shelters. They were good hunters and made powerful stone weapons and tools. They hunted mainly reindeer and bison, but their diet also included fish and shellfish, reptiles, nuts, fruit, roots, bulbs and fungi.

Palaeolithic tools from an eastern European settlement

Burin - a bone scraper for cleaning up animal skins

Bone fish-hook

Bone dagger

Meat was roasted on fires, or cooked in leather bags placed on hot stones. Animal skins were used as clothing and bedding, and to make tents and bags.

ART AND RELIGION

The Palaeolithic people of Europe were the world's first known artists. Wonderful examples of their work, dating from about 18,000BC, have been found in the Lascaux caves in the Dordogne region of France. The cave walls are decorated with vivid hunting scenes of bison, reindeer and horses.

Scattered among pictures of animals at Lascaux are strange geometric signs. No one knows exactly what these mean, but many experts believe they have some religious significance.

Bison, reindeer and horses charge across the cave wall.

Palaeolithic carvings of pregnant women, known as Venus figures, have also been discovered. They were probably symbols of fertility, perhaps for use in religious rituals. These figures have been found all over western and northern Europe. This suggests that religious beliefs were shared by people living over a large area and that the early Europeans had the language to communicate abstract ideas.

There is evidence that spiritual beliefs became more complex as the Stone Age developed. Mesolithic graves have been discovered which show that dead people were decorated with necklaces and sprinkled with red ochre (a red soil). This is thought to represent blood and to symbolize new lives in the afterworld.

Reconstruction of a burial scene

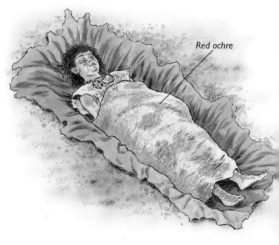

Red ochre

During the Neolithic Age, circles of free-standing stones were built all over western Europe. Many, such as Stonehenge in southern England, still survive. Some were enormous and must have taken hundreds of years to construct. As they appear to have had no practical purpose, experts think that they were probably built as religious monuments.

THE FARMING REVOLUTION

The introduction of farming marks the beginning of the Neolithic Age. It first developed in the Middle East between 9000 and 7000BC, and spread west into Europe in about 6000BC. Farming brought with it enormous changes which had a profound effect on everyday life. People discovered that instead of having to adapt themselves to their environment, they could change their environment to suit themselves. The first step was to learn to domesticate animals (sheep and goats) and to keep them in flocks. Once hunters had become herdsmen, people no longer had to travel over long distances to find food. Later, plants were also brought under control, as farmers began to sow seeds and harvest crops. This new farming way of life meant that people had to stay in one place, so the first permanent communities, or villages, grew up.

Reconstruction of an early farming settlement c.5000BC

Farming families lived in houses which we call long houses.

Pigs

Goats

Walls were made of wooden boards and woven reeds with mud.

Thatch or reed roof

Pig roasting on a spit

Sheep

THE AGE OF METALS

After the Stone Age came the Bronze Age and then the Iron Age. Europeans learned, again from the people of the Middle East, how to extract metal from minerals and to use it to make tools and weapons. By 1000BC, metal had replaced stone as the main material for tools. This meant that farming equipment improved, so more food was produced. As people had more to eat, the population grew. This led to competition for farming land and the outbreak of fighting between rival communities. Knowledge of metalwork was used to make stronger, deadlier weapons, and

Scandinavian bronze figure c.1250BC

communities began to build fortified settlements to keep out hostile intruders.

The metal ages also led to the development of new sophisticated forms of art.

CIVILIZATION BEGINS IN EUROPE

Historians use the term "civilization" to describe a way of life which has reached a highly developed stage. A civilization is usually built up around a city and has its own political and legal systems, its own art and architecture, and a form of writing.

From about 6000BC, farmers settled on the island of Crete and the Greek mainland. These people lived simple lives, but by 2000BC a very distinctive civilization had grown up on Crete. Historians call it Minoan, after Minos, a legendary Cretan king. Minoan civilization was based on a highly organized economy, run from a number of large palaces, often at the heart of well-planned towns. The

Fresco from a Minoan palace, c.1600-1400BC

Minoans developed trading contacts with other ancient peoples, such as the Egyptians.

By 1600BC, a separate civilization had grown up on mainland Greece, based around a group of cities, each ruled by a king. It is called Mycenaean, after Mycenae, the largest city. In about 1450BC, the Mycenaeans invaded Crete and conquered the Minoans. They took over Cretan trade and, until 1250BC, enjoyed a period of increasing wealth. But, by 1050BC, after a series of wars and bad harvests, Mycenaean civilization had collapsed.

Greece then entered a period known as the Dark Ages, when many of the skills they had developed (such as writing) were lost.

Ivory head of a Mycenaean warrior, c.13th century BC

THE GREAT AGE OF GREECE

From about 800BC, a great civilization grew up on the Greek mainland. It reached its peak in the 5th century BC, in a period known as the Classical Age. The influence of Classical Greece survives throughout the modern world and many aspects of European civilization are based on ideas developed at this time.

THE CITY STATES

During the Classical Age, Greek culture was based on city states, which had developed around the old cities of the Mycenaean period (see page 9). Each state, or *polis*, consisted of a city and its surrounding countryside. The largest was Athens, which became a great commercial and cultural capital. Trade was a vital part of the economy. Merchants traded with other peoples around the Mediterranean, including the Egyptians and the Phoenicians (people from what is now Israel, Lebanon and Syria).

A Greek trading ship c.300BC

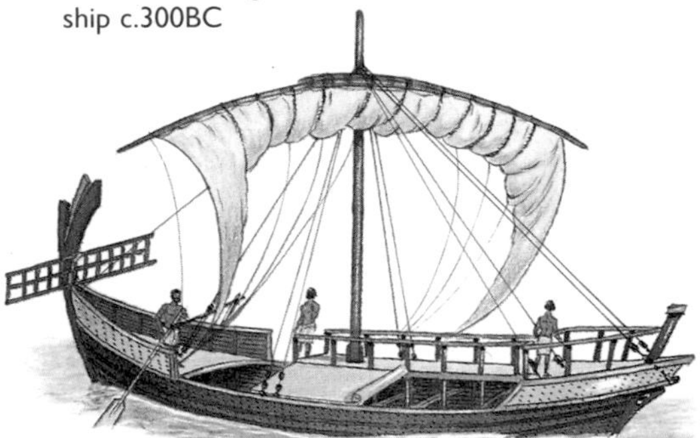

THE BIRTH OF DEMOCRACY

The system of government called democracy, which is the basis of nearly all European governments today, was first developed by the Athenians over 2000 years ago. The word itself comes from the Greek *demos*, meaning "people", and *kratos*, meaning "rule".

During the 6th and 7th centuries BC, Athens, like most city states, was run by a group of rich landowners called aristocrats. But as trade flourished, a class of wealthy traders and merchants emerged, who also demanded a say in running the polis. By 508BC, a new form of government had grown up which allowed all citizens (free males, born in the state) a role in government. Women and slaves were excluded from voting. In a modern democracy, however, all adults in a state can elect the government.

THE GREEK ARMIES

The Greeks were the first Europeans to raise disciplined fighting forces. Each city state had its own army, and wars were frequent. Citizens were expected to fight whenever they were called, but they had to provide their own uniforms and weapons. Richer soldiers, called *hoplites*, had the best equipment and were the most important part of the army.

The Greeks also had a powerful navy. In the 6th century BC, they invented the *trireme*, a warship with three levels of oars on each side of the boat. These were the fastest and most successful ships in the Mediterranean.

A hoplite soldier

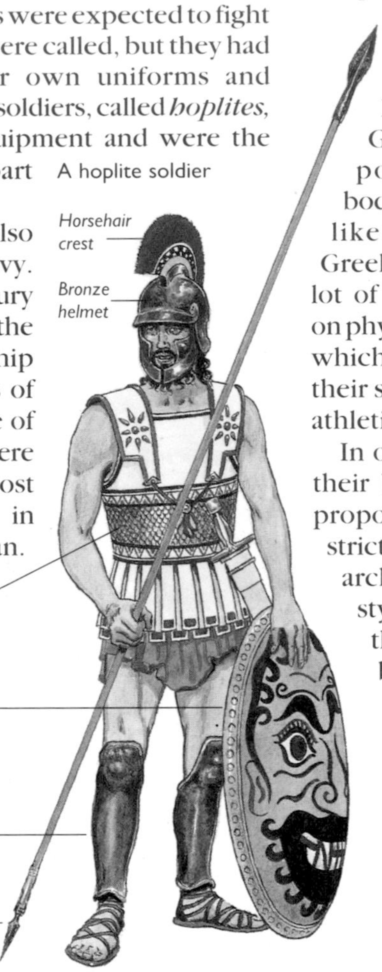

Horsehair crest

Bronze helmet

Bronze and leather breast and back plate

Each hoplite could choose the decoration on his bronze and leather shield.

Bronze leg guards, called greaves, protected the lower parts of the legs.

Spear

PHILOSOPHY AND SCIENCE

The early Greeks made up stories about their gods to explain things they couldn't understand, such as the seasons and the weather. These stories are known as myths. By the Classical Age, however, scholars had started to look for rational explanations for why things happened. These scholars were called philosophers which means lovers of wisdom. They studied mathematics, science and geography, as well as moral questions about how people should behave. Their ideas and methods of study provided many of the foundations for European learning.

SCULPTURE AND ARCHITECTURE

The architecture and sculpture of Classical Greece have had a great influence on European art. Greek sculptors portrayed the body in a very life-like way. The Greeks placed a lot of importance on physical fitness, which is shown in their sculptures of athletic men.

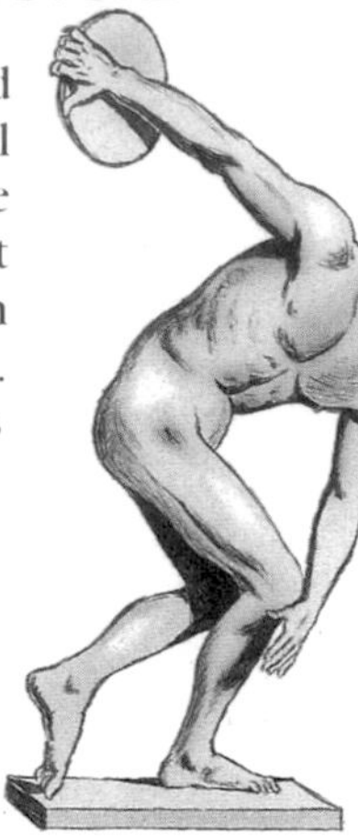

A Roman copy of the Greek statue, *The discus thrower*.

In order to give their buildings a sense of balance and proportion, Greek architects followed strict mathematical rules. Their architecture is divided into two main styles, Doric and Ionic, according to the type of column used. The picture below shows a typical Doric temple. The architectural features shown here were used in many Greek buildings.

This is a reconstruction of the Parthenon, a temple in Athens. It was built by the architect Ictinus between 447BC and 438BC.

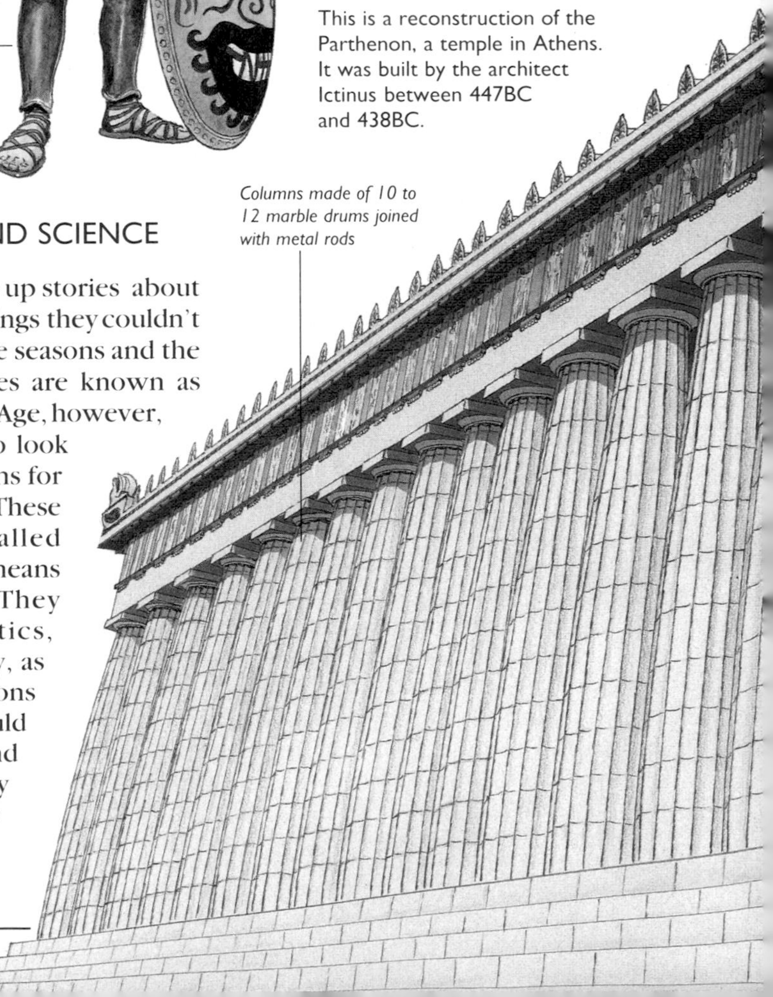

Columns made of 10 to 12 marble drums joined with metal rods

POETRY AND PLAYS

The style and rhythms of Greek poetry have been imitated by poets throughout the ages. Homer (c.9th century BC), the most famous Greek poet, created the earliest surviving examples of European literature. His best-known poems are the *Iliad* and the *Odyssey*, which tell exciting stories about Greek gods and heroes. At first Homer's poems were passed on by word of mouth. They were not written down until centuries after his death.

European theatre also has its roots in Ancient Greece.

Actors wore elaborate masks with exaggerated facial expressions. The masks were made of stiffened fabric or cork.

The first permanent theatres were built there, and the idea of the play itself developed from an annual religious festival celebrating the god Dionysus, for which songs and dances were composed. Greek plays developed into two distinct types: tragedy and comedy. Tragedies were usually stories about heroes and gods. Comedies were not necessarily funny but the characters were ordinary people and the plots dealt with everyday life.

Greek playwrights, such as Sophocles and Euripides, still have a tremendous influence on modern European dramatists.

THE ALPHABET

By 800BC, the Greeks had started to write again - a skill they had lost during the Dark Ages. They adapted a Phoenician script to create their own alphabet. This, in turn, was adapted by the Romans who invented the alphabet which is used in most of Europe today. This table shows ancient Greek letters and their Roman equivalents.

α	β	γ	δ	ε	ζ	η	θ
a	b	g	d	e	z	e	th
ι	κ	λ	μ	ν	ξ	o	π
i	k	l	m	n	x/ks	o	p
ρ	σ	τ	υ	φ	χ	ψ	ω
r	s	t	u	f/ph	ch	ps	o

THE RISE OF ALEXANDER THE GREAT

Rivalry between the city states erupted into the Peloponnesian wars (431-404BC) which tore the Greek world apart. Philip II, king of Macedonia, a kingdom in northern Greece, took advantage of this weakness and embarked on a series of military conquests. By 338BC, he had absorbed most of Greece into his kingdom.

In 336BC, his son "Alexander the Great" inherited the throne and carried on the military traditions of his father. He set out to win an overseas empire for Macedonia and succeeded in conquering vast territories that stretched across the Middle East as far as India.

After Alexander died in 301BC, his empire was divided between rival generals and it was weakened by a series of internal wars. By 146BC, Greece had been taken over by the Roman empire.

The part of a classical building above the columns is called the entablature.

Architrave (the lowest part of the entablature)

Frieze decorated with scenes from mythology

Pediment (the triangular section above the frieze) decorated with sculptures and brightly painted.

Cornice, a ledge around the pediment

Roman mosaic of Alexander the Great

THE LANGUAGES OF EUROPE

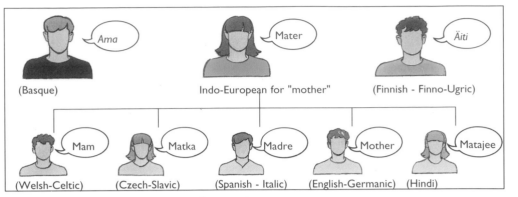

(Basque) — Ama
Mater — Indo-European for "mother"
Äiti — (Finnish - Finno-Ugric)

Mam — (Welsh-Celtic)
Matka — (Czech-Slavic)
Madre — (Spanish - Italic)
Mother — (English-Germanic)
Matajee — (Hindi)

This diagram shows the similarities and differences in the word "mother" in Indo-European and non-Indo-European languagues.

Experts have shown that nearly all European languages originally grew out of a single common one. Linguists can reconstruct this parent language by studying the structures of words in different European languages. We call the parent language Indo-European, but we don't know exactly who the original speakers were or what they called it.

Linguists believe the language was first spoken in southern central Asia. From there, in about 2000BC, the Indo-Europeans began to migrate, splitting up into different language groups as they did so. Some went east into India, while others migrated across Europe. This means that languages like Bengali and Hindi come from the same source as European languages. In Europe, four main language groups developed: Celtic, Italic, Germanic and Slavic. Most modern European languages belong to one of these ancient groups. The diagram above right shows the similarities between words in certain languages.

CELTIC

From the 6th century BC, Celtic tribes colonized Europe. They had their own civilization, based around farming settlements, and a complex religion with a number of gods, many associated with nature and warfare.

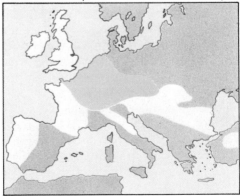

Extent of Celtic speakers before the Roman empire

☐ Celtic heartland, 7th century BC
☐ Extent of Celtic speakers, 250BC

By 250BC, Celtic languages were spoken over a vast area stretching from western Britain and Ireland to southern Russia and Turkey. But these languages did not survive the invasion of the Romans and the later migrations of Germanic speakers.

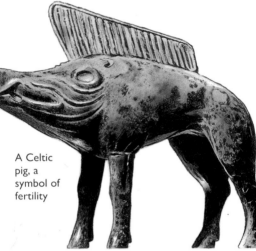

A Celtic pig, a symbol of fertility

Today, only small pockets of Celtic speakers remain, mainly in Brittany (in France), Wales, Scotland and Ireland.

ITALIC

The Romans spoke an Italic language called Latin, which they introduced throughout their expanding empire from the 3rd century BC. As a result, many Celtic languages were wiped out. The inhabitants of the Roman provinces did not learn the official Latin used for law and government, but instead picked up the everyday Latin spoken by soldiers and traders. Local variations developed in different areas. These eventually grew into modern Italic languages, like French and Spanish, which are also known as Romance languages because they are based on the language of the Romans.

GERMANIC AND SLAVIC

Germanic and Slavic languages were spoken mainly beyond the borders of the Roman empire. This enabled them to survive without being swallowed up by Latin. Over the centuries, however, they borrowed many Latin words, because, even after the fall of the empire, Latin remained the language of Christianity and education. So, as Christianity and learning spread, Latin words were adopted by non-Romance languages.

An English religious manuscript with Latin inscriptions

Today, American is the language of popular culture in the same way that Latin was the language of high culture. As a result, many American words are absorbed by other languages.

In the 5th and 6th centuries AD, Germanic people invaded western Europe and destroyed the Roman empire. But they had less success than the Romans in exporting their languages and eventually they adopted local languages themselves.

A night club sign in Paris uses the American word "disco".

Characteristic hairstyle of side-braids and a top-knot

Shield

A throwing-axe called a francisca

Brightly dyed tunic

A Germanic warrior, 5th century AD, who invaded the Roman territory of Gaul.

In England, however, where Latin had never taken hold as an everyday language, the language of the Saxon Germanic invaders was adopted by the local population. It became the basis of modern English. A few Latin words entered the English language via the Christian Church. But it was not until the invasion of the French-speaking Normans in the 11th century (see page 17), that many Latinate forms came into English.

ODD ONES OUT

The only European languages that do not come from Indo-European are Basque, and a group called Finno-Ugric.

Basque is probably Europe's most ancient language. It does not belong to any group and seems to be almost completely unconnected to any other language in the world. It is spoken by over half a million people in the Pyrenees region of Spain and France. Linguists believe that Basque was spoken before the Indo-Europeans arrived in western Europe. It may have survived unaltered because the Basque people led such isolated lives in inaccessible countryside, and so would not have had much contact with either the Celts, the Romans or other invading people.

A Basque mountain settlement in the Pyrenees

There are more than 22 million speakers of Finno-Ugric languages in scattered communities stretching from Norway to Siberia. Like Basque, the origins of the Finno-Ugric languages, which include Finnish, Hungarian and Lapp, are uncertain.

LANGUAGE, NATIONALITY AND NATION STATES

In the 19th century, the idea that national groups (people with a common language and culture) should govern themselves emerged as a powerful political force. During this time many peoples fought for, and won, political independence. For much of Europe's history, however, feelings of nationality were not linked to the idea of nation states.

In 1991, the people of Latvia, Lithuania and Estonia formed a human chain across all three countries as a statement of their independence from the USSR.

This is because much of Europe was made up of small states ruled by large empires (such as the Holy Roman Empire, see page 21). So peoples like the Serbs and Croats felt they had their own nationality (a common culture and language) without their own nation state.

Many of the people who won independence in the 19th century found themselves controlled by the Soviet Union in the 20th century. But the collapse of communism in the early 1990s led to new demands for independence from many national groups.

This statue commemorates the statesman Bismarck who led the German nationalist movement (see

ESPERANTO

Esperanto was created as an international language in the late 19th century by a Polish doctor, Lodovik Lazarus Zamenhof (1859-1917). Although Esperanto belongs to no nation in particular, it is based on a combination of European languages and uses the Roman alphabet. It is easier to learn than other languages, because its grammar and pronunciation are very simple and regular.

The Esperanto logo reads "friendship across borders".

Amikeco trans limoj

ROMAN EUROPE

Bust of Trajan, Roman emperor from AD79-81

For more than six centuries, Europe was dominated by the Romans, who ruled over a vast empire. Many people resented Roman rule, but it did bring peace and prosperity. After the empire collapsed in the 5th century AD, many aspects of Roman life survived. Much of what the countries of Europe have in common today is a result of their shared Roman heritage. Roman civilization was itself influenced by Greece, and both cultures are together described as classical.

The Roman empire grew out of a few farming settlements established around the River Tiber in Italy, in the 8th century BC. These expanded into the city of Rome, which was to become the heart of the empire and headquarters of the Christian church (see page 18).

THE BIRTH OF THE REPUBLIC

In the early days, Rome was ruled by kings. But, in 510BC, the Romans drove the last king out of the city and Rome became a republic, a state governed by representatives of the people. The heads of influential families made up a ruling body called the Senate. The Senate passed laws and looked after the running of the Republic. Every two years, two senators were elected by Roman citizens to head the government. At first, citizenship was granted only to men of Roman parents, but later it was extended to include certain non-Romans in the empire.

Senators debating in the Senate

The Roman Republic inspired later political movements, such as the French Revolution and the North American struggle for independence. Many states adopted the Roman name, the Senate, for their senior law-making body.

ROMAN EXPANSION

The Romans built up one of the greatest armies in the ancient world. By the mid 3rd century BC they had conquered most of Italy. In 146BC, they destroyed the city of Carthage in North Africa and took control of the Carthaginian empire. This included lands in Sicily, North Africa and Spain. The Romans continued to expand both north and east, eventually absorbing the civilizations of Greece and later Egypt. By the beginning of the 2nd century AD, the empire had reached its greatest extent. It stretched from the Persian Gulf in the east, to the Atlantic Ocean in the west, and from North Africa to southern Scotland (see map).

A winged goddess, a Roman symbol of military victory

FROM REPUBLIC TO EMPIRE

As the empire grew in size, there were bitter disputes among senators about how it should be run. In 46BC, a general called Julius Caesar seized power and became sole ruler. Two years later, he was assassinated. Civil wars raged until 31BC, when Caesar's great-nephew Octavian won an important battle and rose to power. He became the most powerful leader Rome had ever known, changing his name to Augustus, meaning "revered one". Although he did not give himself the title, Augustus was in fact the first Roman emperor. His rule marks the beginning of the period known as the Roman Empire.

Augustus created a system of government in which the emperor and Senate could work together. But this broke down under his successors, and plots and counter-plots made government in Rome impossible. A more stable period of prosperity and military success followed in AD68, when Vespasian became emperor. This continued under the emperors Titus, Trajan and Hadrian.

RUNNING THE EMPIRE

The Roman empire was divided into areas called provinces. Each province was administered by a Roman governor, who represented the Republic or, later, the emperor. Their job was to collect taxes, introduce Roman law and act as judges in important trials. They were supported by the army, which was there to crush any rebellions against Roman rule.

The Roman legal system survived the fall of the empire, and during the Middle Ages was adopted in many European kingdoms. In 1804, the French legal system was restructured following the ancient Roman model.

This is a signifer, a standard-bearer of the Roman army. Every legion (a unit of about 4200 soldiers) had its own signifer who carried a pole bearing the legion's emblems.

— Standard

Signifers often wore a lion skin over their heads and backs to make them look more frightening.

Sporran or groin-guard

Tunics were made of wool or linen.

Leather sandals

ROMAN TECHNOLOGY

The Romans were skilled engineers and introduced many technological advances throughout their empire. Towns had piped water supplies and sewage systems and some houses had central heating. Travel was made easy by a network of roads that stretched over 85,000km (50,000 miles). This enabled the army to march swiftly to troublespots and encouraged trade between provinces. Today, some Roman roads can still be seen as ruins, but many more form the foundation of modern roads and railways. After the empire declined, many engineering skills were forgotten and not revived until the 19th century.

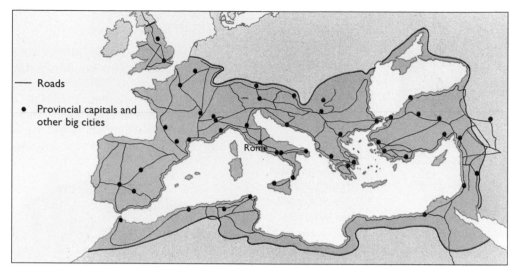

— Roads

• Provincial capitals and other big cities

Rome

The extent of the Roman empire, 2nd century AD

This picture shows the Romans building an aqueduct to carry water to a provincial town.

Some aqueducts were over 80km (50 miles) long.

Cranes and pulleys lifted heavy slabs of stone to the top of the aqueduct.

The water was carried in this channel.

Hundreds of slaves were used on these massive building projects.

THE DECLINE OF ROME

As the Roman empire grew larger, governors in the provinces relied more and more on the army to keep control. As a result, the army became very powerful and started choosing and deposing emperors as it saw fit, sometimes even offering the position to the highest bidder. This led to civil wars. The empire was left open to attack from tribes, known as barbarians, who lived on the borders of the empire.

Emperor Diocletian (AD284-305) tried to restore stability by dividing the government of the empire in half under two separate emperors. By 395, the split had become permanent, with a Western empire, ruled from Rome, and an Eastern empire, ruled from Constantinople (now Istanbul). But this division could not save the Romans. In the 5th century, barbarians began occupying parts of the Western empire. In AD410 and AD455, Rome was sacked (destroyed and plundered) and in AD476, the Western Roman empire finally came to an end.

Half-circle scaffolding was used to support arches.

Shield, helmet and spear of a Germanic horseman

From the 2nd century BC, tribes known as Germani settled around the northern borders of the Roman empire. Over several hundred years, they lived in relative peace with the Romans. But, in the 5th century AD, a warlike tribe called the Huns advanced from the borders of China right into eastern Europe. They seized the land of the Germanic tribes, who in turn were pushed west into conflict with the Romans. Roman forces could not withstand the continual attacks and the empire began to crumble. Finally, Rome itself was invaded and destroyed. In AD476, Romulus Augustulus, the last emperor of the Western Roman empire, was deposed.

The collapse of Roman civilization shattered the political, cultural and social unity of Europe. Most of the Western empire was divided into small kingdoms ruled by Germanic kings (see map below). But many of these kingdoms were short-lived. For several centuries, Europe was in turmoil as war-like tribes migrated across the continent fighting each other. Some historians call this period Europe's "Dark Ages".

The Germanic kingdoms (c.493)

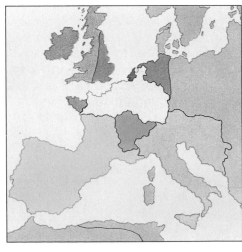

⬛ Angle and Saxon lands	
⬜ Ostrogoth	⬛ Vandal
⬜ Visigoth	⬛ Burgundian
⬜ Frankish	⬛ Celtic

THE BYZANTINE EMPIRE

The Eastern Roman empire (see page 15), which became known as the Byzantine empire, struggled on for another 1000 years after the fall of Rome. But it was continually under attack from Muslim Arabs and Turks and it slowly shrank in size. In 1453,

the capital, Constantinople, finally fell to the Turks and became part of their Ottoman empire (see page 19).

Although constantly threatened with invasion, the Byzantine empire became an important cultural focus for eastern Europeans and helped to preserve classical learning and Christianity in the East. It grew away from its Roman roots, however, and a distinct Byzantine culture grew up.

Greek rather than Latin became the official language and a separate Eastern Catholic church developed, with its own form of worship and its own style of art and architecture. The religious and cultural traditions of the Byzantines were inherited by the Greeks and the Slavs.

Byzantine churches were decorated with lavish mosaics, made of precious stones, metals and small pieces of stained glass.

THE RISE OF THE FRANKS

One of the most successful of the Germanic kingdoms was that of Clovis the Frank (481-511). He expanded his territory until his kingdom was the largest and most powerful in the region. Although his kingdom was divided and weakened after his death, its fortunes were revived in 771, when power passed to his descendant Charlemagne.

Charlemagne was a brilliant soldier and a devout Christian. He built up an extensive empire (see the map shown on the right) and converted the pagans (non-Christians) that he conquered to Christianity. His greatest ambition was to unite all Christian lands under a second Roman Empire, with himself as ruler. Although he

A carving of Emperor Charlemagne from his tomb

Extent of Charlemagne's empire c.814

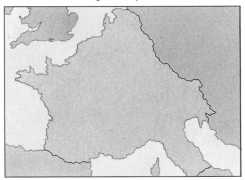

never achieved this, he was given the title of "Emperor of the Romans" by the Pope on Christmas Day 800. But he was not nearly as powerful as the Ancient Roman emperors had been.

After his death, Charlemagne's empire was split into two much weaker parts (an Eastern and a Western kingdom), and the Franks lost their influence in Europe. But the ideal of a Christian Roman empire survived him. In 962, Otto I, the king of the Eastern kingdom (roughly the area of modern Germany), was crowned Holy Roman Emperor and became the founder of the Holy Roman Empire. This title survived in Europe until 1806, although for much of this time it meant very little.

THE SLAVS AND THE PEOPLE FROM THE STEPPES

The Slavs were an Indo-European people who had settled in the Pripet Marshes around the River Dnieper, in what is today the Ukraine. Between the 6th and the 9th centuries, their settled lifestyle was disrupted by the westward migration of nomadic tribesmen from the Steppes (grassy plains in Central Asia). The first invaders were the Avars who, in 552, drove the Slavs from their homeland and left them scattered across eastern Europe. Further invasions followed and, for the next few hundred years, eastern Europe was in disarray. Small kingdoms were created, only to be destroyed by rival tribes or taken over by more powerful states, such as the Byzantine empire.

By the 9th century, however, the area had become more stable. The Slavs had settled in new territories, and were becoming politically organized. Many converted to Christianity. Through intermarriage and community life, the Steppes invaders were gradually becoming absorbed into Slav society. New independent Slav states were founded in Bulgaria (716), Croatia (815), Moravia (830) and Poland (960).

VIKING RAIDERS AND TRADERS

The Vikings (also known as Northmen or Norsemen) were seafaring people from Scandinavia. From the 8th to the 11th centuries, they terrorized western Europe by carrying out violent raids. They robbed and plundered villages and monasteries, taking home cattle and treasures.

Not all Viking expeditions were raids, however. Swedish Vikings, known as Varangians, settled as traders around the Baltic coast. From here they moved southward and mingled with the local Slav population. In about 862, Rurik, head of the Rus tribe of Varangians, founded a state called Russia around the city of Novgorod. Rurik's successors expanded the territory and moved the Russian capital to Kiev. Kiev became a major city and the capital of the first Russian empire.

Danish Vikings sailed west and south,

and settled in eastern England and in parts of northern France. The French called the invaders Normans. In return for a promise of peace, the French king made the Norman leader a duke and gave him some territory, which became known as Normandy. In 1066, a Norman duke, later known as William the Conqueror, sailed to England and defeated Harold, the last Saxon king, at the Battle of Hastings. William became the first Norman king of England.

For centuries, people thought that the first European to reach America was the Italian explorer Christopher Columbus in 1492. But, in fact, Vikings had been there nearly five centuries earlier. In the

9th century, Norwegian Vikings, under the command of Leif Ericsson, crossed the Atlantic Ocean and became the first Europeans to set foot on American soil.

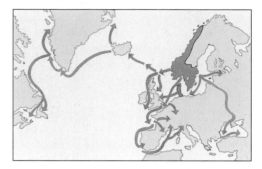

The Vikings were skilled navigators and shipbuilders. They built long, narrow ships, known as longboats, which were strong enough to weather ocean storms.

Decorative posts were attached to each end of the keel (the backbone of the ship).

Longboats were powered by the wind or by rowing.

The mast fitted into a heavy piece of wood called the mastblock, which was attached to the keel.

Rudder, a large wooden paddle for steering

CHRISTIAN EUROPE

The Christian religion has been very important in Europe's development. After being adopted by the Romans in the 4th century, it spread rapidly throughout their empire. During the Middle Ages, Europe was sometimes known as Christendom, because the continent was united by its Christian faith. At this time, the Church had its own courts, collected its own taxes, and had a great deal of control over people's daily lives. The Church's importance was reflected in the many magnificent cathedrals and churches that were built during this period. Although Christianity is no longer so widely observed in Europe, much of what people think is right or wrong, as well as many European laws, are based on the teachings of the Christian religion.

Milan Cathedral (c.1385-1485). The features labelled here are characteristic of medieval Gothic architecture (see page 49).

The body of the church is about 43m (145ft) high, not including the tower and the spire.

Roof made of massive marble slabs

Pinnacles crowned with statues

Spire

Tower

Tall stained glass windows

THE ORIGINS OF CHRISTIANITY

Christianity began in Palestine, in the Middle East, with a Jew called Jesus of Nazareth (c.4BC-AD30), later known as Jesus Christ. Jesus proclaimed himself the son of God and preached that all people were equal. He was arrested and crucified (nailed to a cross to die) by the Roman authorities who ruled Palestine. His followers, known as disciples, believed that he rose from the dead.

This 5th century Italian mosaic shows Christ as a shepherd looking after his sheep.

After Jesus's death, Christianity was preached to both Jews and Gentiles (non-Jews). Despite persecution from the Romans (arrest, torture and often death), the new religion spread rapidly, especially among the poor.

THE EARLY CHURCH

After the Roman emperor, Constantine, converted to Christianity in 312, a highly organized church grew up under the leadership of bishops. The most important was the bishop of Rome, later called the Pope.

When non-Christian tribes conquered the Roman empire, the Church looked threatened. But large numbers of men, known as missionaries, were sent out to convert the conquerors, and Christianity was kept alive.

The Church, however, became divided between the Catholic Church, based in Rome, and the Orthodox Church, based in Constantinople. In the 9th century, Orthodox missionaries, under St. Cyril, were sent to convert the Slavs in Russia and eastern Europe. Later, rival Catholic missionaries persuaded the western Slavs to change their allegiance to Rome.

This script is the Cyrillic alphabet. It is a version of the Greek alphabet adapted by Christian converts for Slav languages and named after St. Cyril. It is still used in Russia.

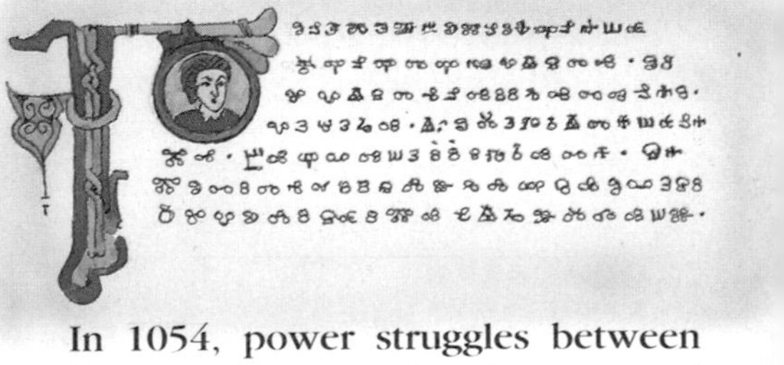

In 1054, power struggles between religious leaders in Rome and Constantinople led to an official split between the two Churches.

MONASTICISM

This picture, from a medieval manuscript, shows monks carrying out their daily tasks.

In 4th century Egypt, some devout Christians began to withdraw from everyday life in order to dedicate themselves to God. At first they lived alone, but later they formed into communities: monasteries for monks (men) and convents for nuns (women). In the 6th century, monasteries spread to Europe where St. Benedict of Nursia (in Italy) introduced a set of rules which laid down how monks and nuns should live. By the 8th century, religious communities had been established all over Europe. As well as being places of prayer, monasteries also acted as hospitals, schools and hostels.

CHURCH AGAINST STATE

In the 11th century, the Pope declared that he was superior to all non-religious rulers. The kings of Europe vigorously opposed such claims, and clashes between the Church and medieval states were common. Matters came to a head in 1303, when the French king imprisoned the Pope and moved the headquarters of the Church to Avignon, France. Between 1309 and 1377, a series of French popes was elected under the direct influence of the French kings.

In 1378, the Church was returned to Rome, but it never regained its former political power.

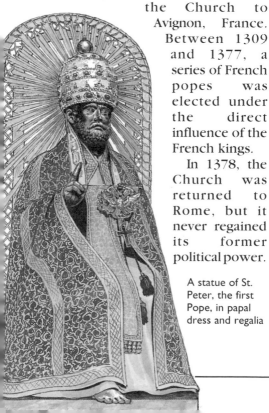

A statue of St. Peter, the first Pope, in papal dress and regalia

ISLAM: THE CHALLENGE FROM THE EAST

The religion of Islam was founded in Arabia by a man called Mohammed (c.570-632), who claimed that he was a prophet (someone who could speak for God on Earth). By the time of his death, Islam had spread over much of the Middle East. Mohammed's followers, known as Muslims, built up a large empire. This included territory in Spain and Portugal, some of which was held until the 15th century.

By the 11th century, the Middle East was dominated by a Muslim people called Turks, who had migrated west from central Asia. In 1071, the Turks captured Palestine (holy land for both Christians and

This soldier belongs to the Teutonic Order, a special orders of monks set up to fight the crusades.

Islamic warrior

Muslims) from the Byzantines. This sparked off the Crusades, a series of military campaigns by Europe against the Turks. After the First Crusade (1096-99), a Christian state was set up in Palestine. But later crusades were less successful and, in 1291, the Christians were forced from the area.

In the 13th century, a group of Turks called the Ottomans founded a new and powerful empire. In 1453, the Ottomans captured Constantinople and the Byzantine empire was overthrown. They went on to conquer lands in eastern Europe, where they held some lands until the 19th century.

THE REFORMATION

Martin Luther preaching

In the 16th century, a German monk named Martin Luther (1483-1546) began to criticize strongly the corruption he saw in the Roman Catholic Church. His criticism grew into attacks on Church teachings and even on the supremacy of the Pope himself. This developed into a movement called the Reformation, which led to the founding of Protestant (non-Catholic) churches.

Luther was expelled from the Catholic Church and founded his own Lutheran Church. In 1525, Lutheranism became the official religion of Saxony (a state in the Holy Roman Empire), from where it spread to other German states. Reformation leaders, such as Calvin, a Frenchman, and Zwingli, a Swiss priest, also founded their own Protestant churches. Calvinism was stricter than Lutheranism, and better organized, and it made many converts. Calvinist

communities grew up in France, Holland, Switzerland and parts of eastern Europe.

In an attempt to win back its followers, the Catholic Church introduced reforms. A meeting held at Trento (in northern Italy) from 1545 made plans to stamp out corruption in the clergy. It also reaffirmed the supremacy of the Pope and launched a campaign to reconvert Protestants. Throughout Europe there was religious persecution and warfare, as the two sides competed for control. Europe became permanently divided between Protestantism and Catholicism.

Churches in Europe, 1560

THE MIDDLE AGES

A medieval peasant farmer

The period in Europe from about 1000 to 1500 is known as the Middle Ages. During this time, most Europeans lived as farmers, although under a system called feudalism (see below) only the wealthy owned land. Religion played an important part in people's lives and, in western Europe, the Roman Catholic Church was a powerful political force. Europe was divided into kingdoms, ruled by kings or dukes. But, particularly in the early part of the period, it was often local chiefs who held real power. Wars were frequent, as rulers fought to keep control or to win more territory.

HOW FEUDALISM DEVELOPED

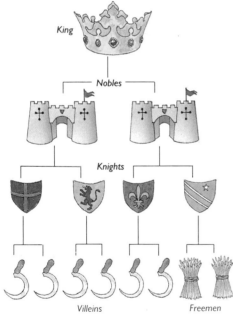

This diagram shows the hierarchy in feudal society.

The break up of Charlemagne's empire and the Viking raids brought disruption to western Europe. Both peasants and kings looked to powerful warriors for protection. In return for their help, these warriors were rewarded with large estates. This is the origin of the European nobility. A system of rights and duties grew up between these nobles (the feudal lords) and those they protected (their vassals). It ensured that everyone in a community was defended. This system is called feudalism and it reached its peak in the 11th and 12th centuries.

At the top of the feudal system was the king. He gave land to the nobles in return for an oath of loyalty and their promise to provide soldiers (called knights) in times of war. The nobles gave land to knights, in return for their services as soldiers. Villeins were people who worked on the estates of the nobles and knights, and were given a small plot of land for themselves, in return for protection. They were unable to leave the estate without the permission of the landowner and had to pay him rents and dues. Some peasants were freemen. This meant they paid rent for their lands, but were not tied to the estate and could leave if they wished.

THE GROWTH OF TOWNS AND TRADE

Merchants and craftsmen did not fit into the feudal system, but lived by selling their skills or goods for money. They tended to settle together in market towns.

By the 11th century, merchants and craftsmen had organized themselves into guilds. These were a bit like modern trade unions. Each guild regulated prices and wages, set standards of work and looked after its members.

Guild badge of the Fishermen of Zurich

As trade grew, towns developed into cities. In many places, kings and nobles sold charters to the guilds, allowing them to to rule the city. By 1500, some of the great cities in Italy, such as Florence and Venice, had become independent states with their own governments.

A complex economy soon developed throughout Europe. In the 13th century, the first European banking system was introduced by Italian people, called the Lombards. They soon set up a network of banks all over Europe.

The importance of cities and the widespread use of money began to threaten the feudal system. A class of soldiers, called mercenaries, grew up. Unlike knights, they fought for payment and not for land or duty. At the same time more and more peasants became freemen, which meant they owed no obligation to a feudal lord.

Great hall

Chapel

The more powerful feudal lords lived in magnificent castles. This is a 14th century English castle.

Gatehouse

Venice in 1483: a prosperous merchant city

Servants' quarters

Towers strengthened the castle wall and were good look-out posts.

Within the castle walls, vegetables were grown and animals were kept.

Sentries

Private quarters of the lord and his family

THE BIRTH OF PARLIAMENTS

For much of the Middle Ages, feudal lords held real power. They were often more powerful than the kings they were supposed to serve. In 1215, the nobles of England even forced the king to sign a charter, called the *Magna Carta,* which limited his authority over them.

But in the late 13th century, the monarchs of western Europe began to curb the power of the

feudal lords. In England, France and Spain, they did this by inviting the churchmen, knights and townsmen to send representatives to meetings about government and taxes. These meetings gradually became a permanent part of government, and grew into institutions such as Parliament in England, the Estates-General in France and the Cortes in Spain. With the support of these assemblies, the kings were able to raise taxes from all their subjects directly, without going through the feudal lords. This enabled them to pay for their own armies, which meant they were no longer dependent on the lords for protection. By the 16th century, the feudal system had virtually disappeared. People generally felt more loyalty to their king and nation than to their feudal superior and local community.

A Florentine mercenary captain, taken from a painting by Andrea del Castagno

THE HOLY ROMAN EMPIRE

Until the mid 13th century, the Holy Roman Empire, or the Kingdom of Germany as it was also known, was the most powerful force in Europe. At its height in the 12th century, the Holy Roman emperors ruled over territories stretching from the Baltic to Sicily. They had great influence over the Church, choosing their own bishops and sometimes even controlling the elections of Popes. Unlike the other kings in western Europe, however, they never succeeded in breaking the power of the local lords. As the feudal

___ Boundary of the Empire 1125-1254

☐ Sphere of imperial influence

system broke down, imperial authority dwindled rather than increased. By the 16th century, many states in the Empire had become highly efficient independent units, over which the emperor had little control.

THE BLACK DEATH

In 1347, a plague, known as the Black Death, swept through Europe. It raged until 1353 and killed as many as 20 million Europeans. Victims were covered with black swellings which oozed blood and gave unbearable pain until death. Many towns saw half their population die, and some villages were left completely deserted. For example, the population of Florence in Italy fell from 110,000 in 1338 to 50,000 in 1351. The disease was probably spread by deadly parasites found in the stomachs of fleas that lived in the fur of rats.

This illustration from a medieval manuscript shows people burning the clothes of the dead, in an attempt to stop the spread of infection.

THE RENAISSANCE

The word renaissance literally means "rebirth". It is the name given to a great age of European culture at the end of the Middle Ages, when there was a revival of interest in classical civilizations and a new thirst for knowledge about the world. The movement reached its peak in the 15th century in Italian cities such as Florence. From there it spread throughout western Europe.

THE ARTS

Inspired by Greek and Roman statues, Renaissance sculptors aimed to present the human body more realistically. New techniques were discovered, which made paintings look more life-like.

Raphael's The School of Athens 1509-10

For example, artists learned that objects appeared to get smaller the farther away they were from the viewer. This enabled them to give a feeling of depth to their pictures. Renaissance architects used classical features, such as columns, arches and domes. Renaissance literature also imitated classical styles. One of the greatest Renaissance writers was the Italian poet, Petrarch (1304-74).

This Italian villa, known as the Rotunda, by the Renaissance architect, Andrea Palladio (1508-80), has many classical features.

Classical Roman domed roof

Classical facade of columns and entablature (see page 11)

LEONARDO DA VINCI: RENAISSANCE MAN

Many thinkers during the Renaissance believed in the ideal of "universal man": someone who combined a wide range of talents and interests. The Italian painter, Leonardo da Vinci, born in Florence in 1452, typified this ideal. As well as being one of the world's finest painters, Leonardo was also a sculptor, musician, architect, scientist and ingenious inventor.

This is a reconstruction of a flying machine based on designs in Leonardo's sketchbooks.

Beech wood struts

The wings were to be made of a heavy material called taffeta, which had been stiffened in starch.

Sketch of a design for a mechanical wing

His sketchbooks also show detailed drawings of human anatomy.

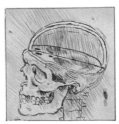

System of cranks and pulleys

The materials Leonardo planned to use would have made his machine weigh about 295kg (650lbs) - too heavy to get off the ground.

The wings were to be powered by the feet working a crank and pulley system, so they flapped up and down.

HUMANISM

The Renaissance also changed people's way of thinking. Throughout the Middle Ages, the Church had stressed human sins and weaknesses. During the Renaissance, a movement grew up, which we call humanism, which stressed human potential and ability. It grew out of the study of the great heroes of the Classical Age (such as Alexander the Great) but developed into a thirst for fresh knowledge. Schools and universities were set up and new scientific and medical research was carried out. The new printing presses meant that new knowledge and ideas could be passed easily between scholars across the continent (see page 46).

Each wing would have been 11m (36ft) long by 3.2m (10.5ft) wide.

NEW HORIZONS

A 15th century compass card

During the Middle Ages, European knowledge of the rest of the world was limited to the north and west coasts of Africa, and the overland trade routes to India and China. Europeans did not know that the huge land mass of North and South America even existed. By 1500, however, their picture was becoming more complete.

This explorer's map of 1489 shows first-hand experience of the West African coast, but no knowledge of America.

During the 15th century, overland routes to India were often blocked by Muslim Turks. Finding a sea route became of great importance, as Europe's economy relied on the luxury trade from the East. Prince Henry of Portugal led the way by funding many voyages. In 1488, Bartholmeu Diaz reached the Cape of Good Hope and, in 1498, Vasco da Gama reached India by sailing around Africa.

CHRISTOPHER COLUMBUS

The Italian explorer Christopher Columbus was convinced that it would be quicker to reach Asia by sailing west, rather than east around Africa. It was a revolutionary idea because many people believed the earth was flat. In 1492, employed by the Spanish king and queen, he set off from Spain. About five weeks later, Columbus landed in the West Indies (a group of islands off the South American coast). Further Spanish expeditions followed and, a few years later, they reached the South American mainland. At first people believed that these lands were part of Asia, and that Columbus had sailed right around the globe. But when explorers from Portugal, Spain, Britain and France also sailed west in search of new sea routes to China and India, it soon became clear that this was not Asia. Instead a whole new continent had been reached. The new discoveries became known as the New World.

This is the *Santa Maria*, the flagship of Columbus's first voyage across the Atlantic.

15th century astrolabe used for determining latitude

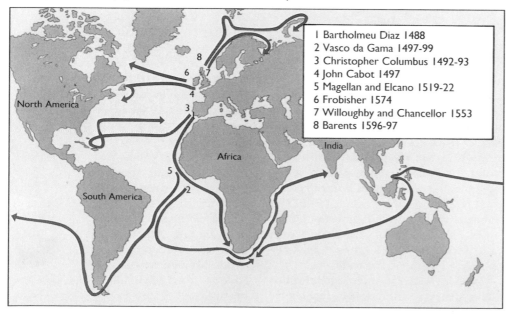

This map shows the voyages of some of the most famous explorers.

North America
Africa
India
South America

1 Bartholmeu Diaz 1488
2 Vasco da Gama 1497-99
3 Christopher Columbus 1492-93
4 John Cabot 1497
5 Magellan and Elcano 1519-22
6 Frobisher 1574
7 Willoughby and Chancellor 1553
8 Barents 1596-97

DIVIDING THE SPOILS

The early explorers returned from the New World laden with gold and silver. Impressed by these riches, Spanish and Portuguese conquerors, known as *conquistadores*, sailed west in search of land and treasures. The Portuguese occupied Brazil, and many became rich growing sugar, cotton and tobacco on vast plantations. The Spanish founded states in Peru and Mexico, both rich in silver, but in doing so destroyed the native civilizations of the Incas and the Aztecs. The natives (called Indians by the Europeans) were used as slaves and many died from overwork or from European diseases.

The *conquistadores* had to pay taxes to their governments back in Europe, so European rulers profited from the discovery of the New World. Charles V of Spain used South American silver to pay for a series of wars against his rivals, winning much new territory as a result.

In the 17th century, colonies were set up in North America by English and French settlers, looking not so much for riches but for a new way of life. Many were fleeing religious persecution.

This Aztec belongs to an elite warrior class, the eagle knights, who wear bright animal costumes in battle.

THE AGE OF KINGS

This crown decorates the throne of Frederick II of Prussia

From the 16th century, European monarchs grew in power. Many began to ignore their great nobles and their parliaments and to make important decisions alone. In France, for example, after 1614 the king no longer called the Estates-General (see page 21). Some rulers, known as absolute monarchs, claimed that their authority came from God and that anyone who challenged their rule was breaking God's law. Austria, France, Russia, Spain, Sweden, Britain and many German states were all ruled by absolute monarchs for a time.

THE BALANCE OF POWER

In the first half of the 16th century, Europe was dominated by Charles V, a member of the Hapsburg family, who had inherited both the Kingdom of Spain and the Holy Roman Empire. Charles built up a powerful army and began to win new lands. His increasing strength forced the other nations of western Europe to band together to curb his military advances. This was the beginning of a political system known as the balance of power. Its aim was to prevent any one nation from becoming so strong that it could overwhelm the rest. If one country looked threatening, the others would unite and form an alliance against it. The most influential nations involved in this system were known as the great powers.

The empire of Charles V, 1519-56

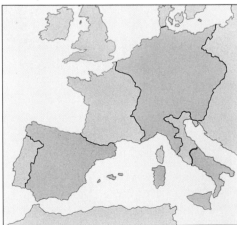

In the 17th century, there were five great powers: France, Austria and Spain (divided between two Hapsburg rulers), Great Britain and the United Provinces of the Netherlands. (The Austrian king was also Holy Roman Emperor, but he had little authority over the German states.)

LOUIS XIV OF FRANCE

In the second half of the 17th century, Louis XIV of France became the most important king in Europe. He won a series of military victories, which extended France's boundaries. The other powers feared his ambitions and formed leagues against him, but France's domination lasted for over a century.

This emblem comes from the main gate of Louis's palace at Versailles. It portrays Louis as the "Sun King", radiating glory.

Louis XIV was also the cultural leader of Europe. His palace at Versailles, just outside Paris, became the model for royal palaces throughout the continent. It was renowned for its grandeur and was designed to make Louis appear to be the most magnificent king in Europe. Great crystal chandeliers hung from the ceilings, their candlelight reflected in gilded mirrors. Fine tapestries and paintings recording Louis's military victories decorated the walls.

The court entertainment at Versailles was legendary. The latest comedies by

The Hall of Mirrors, a reception room at Versailles

the French playwright Molière were performed, and music was specially composed by the most well-known composers of the day.

THE RISE OF PRUSSIA

In the 15th century, Brandenburg was just a small insignificant state in the northeast corner of the Holy Roman Empire. But, by the 17th century, it had gained new territory within the Empire and acquired the state of Prussia (a weak duchy just outside the Empire). In 1701, Brandenburg's ruler, known as the Elector, felt he needed a new title to mark his status as ruler of such a large area. With the Emperor's consent, he was crowned Frederick I, King of Prussia. From this time, all his lands, including Brandenburg, were known as Prussia. In 1742, the other powers had to acknowledge Prussia's strength when Frederick II invaded the Austrian territory of Silesia. After six years of war, the Austrian army was defeated by the disciplined Prussian forces and Silesia became part of Prussia.

A Prussian soldier, 1740

THE RISE OF RUSSIA

From the 11th century, Russia was made up of a number of small states, each ruled by a prince. But in the 13th century, their independence came to an end when the country was conquered by Mongols, a nomadic people from the northeast part of the Steppes now called Mongolia. The Russian princes were forced to pay them tribute in the form of money.

Throughout the 15th century, however, the princes of Muscovy (also known as Moscow) grew in power. They eventually defeated the Mongols and gradually took over the other Russian states. In 1480, Ivan III (the Great) of Moscow declared himself Tsar (sole ruler) of all Russia. But he had an ill-equipped and undisciplined army, and much of his vast empire was inhabited by people over whom he had little control.

In the late 17th century, the Russians acquired a powerful new ruler. Tsar Peter the Great (1682-1725) built up a strong modern army and won brilliant victories against Sweden and Turkey. He also introduced many new industries, improved education and built himself a new city, called St. Petersburg, which followed the latest styles of western European architecture. Russia emerged as one of the great European powers of the 18th and 19th centuries.

THE ENLIGHTENMENT

Bust of Voltaire (1694-1778)

A new intellectual movement, called the Enlightenment, developed in Europe in the 18th century. At its heart was a belief in the power of human reason. Enlightened thinkers believed that people could unravel the mysteries of the universe by means of rational study. The Enlightenment stimulated a new interest in science. As a result many important discoveries were made and invention flourished during this period.

The Enlightenment challenged the Church by encouraging the idea that people could find things out for themselves, without the help of a priest or the Bible. Although many enlightened thinkers were Christian, others, such as the French writer Voltaire, attacked Christianity as an irrational system of beliefs, based on superstition. He argued that it led to prejudice and persecution.

A number of Europe's monarchs, such as Frederick II of Prussia and Catherine the Great of Russia, claimed to support the new trends. They presented themselves as followers of reason and servants of their people, rather than representatives of God. In reality, however, they did little to find out what their subjects wanted.

The Great Palace, built for Peter the Great outside St. Petersburg, was inspired by Versailles.

This picture shows Pilâtre de Rozier and the Marquis d'Arlandes making the first human ascent in a hot air balloon (1783). The balloon was designed by the French inventors Joseph and Etienne Montgolfier.

PEOPLE POWER

While most European states moved towards absolute monarchy, in the United Provinces (also known as the Dutch Republic) and Britain, the middle class gained more influence in government.

The United Provinces were founded in 1588, after the Dutch won independence from Spain. Although a Dutch prince was "head of the state", most power rested with the elected representatives of the Dutch parliament, called the Estates-General.

In Britain, there was a struggle for power between the king, Charles I, and Parliament, which erupted into civil war in 1642. The king was executed in 1649 and Britain briefly became a republic. Although a new king was crowned in 1660, his

A Parliamentarian soldier

A Royalist soldier

The two sides in the civil war

power was limited. Parliament played an ever larger role in government, especially in setting taxes.

WITHDRAWN

REVOLUTION AND NATIONALISM

In 1789, a revolution took place in France in which the monarchy and ruling class were overthrown. This was to have a profound effect on the rest of Europe.

In the 1780s, all the social classes in France were discontented. The nobles, who had been reduced to pampered puppets under Louis XIV, wanted once again to assert control. A growing middle class of businessmen resented being treated as inferiors by the nobles and wanted political power themselves. The poor were suffering from a series of bad harvests.

King Louis XVI (1774-1792) was bankrupt and

The Storming of the Bastille, July 14, 1789

weak. He needed to raise more taxes to pay his debts, but the nobles refused to cooperate. In May 1789, faced with general opposition, Louis decided to summon the Estates-General, a national parliament made up of representatives of the three "estates": the clergy, the nobility and commoners (in practice, the middle class). It soon became clear that the Third Estate (the middle class) would always be outvoted by the other two. So, on June 17, they formed their own National Assembly. This move marked the start of the French Revolution.

Stories soon swept Paris that the king was going to ban the Assembly. On July 14, an angry crowd stormed the Bastille, a prison which had come to symbolize the power of the king and nobility. As the Parisian mob grew increasingly violent, the king was forced to recognize the Assembly and sign a series of declarations stripping the nobility and clergy of their privileges. In 1791, the Assembly imposed a constitution which took away the king's powers. It was then replaced by the National Convention which declared France a republic in 1792. On January 21, 1793, Louis XVI was executed by guillotine for treason.

There were in fact only seven inmates of the prison that day.

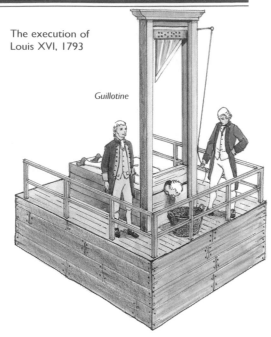

The execution of Louis XVI, 1793

Guillotine

THE TERROR

A violent civil war followed, as republicans fought royalists. In 1793, power passed to a group called the Jacobins, led by Maximilien Robespierre. A period began, known as the Terror, during which anyone suspected of opposing the revolution was put to death.

Many people fled the country in fear of their lives. In Paris, public executions were carried out by guillotine, which became a symbol of the brutality of the Jacobins. Eventually, Robespierre himself was executed in 1794. The Jacobins were replaced by a more moderate government called the Directory.

The army abandoned the king and fought with the people.

The revolutionaries were known as "sans-culottes" meaning "without breeches", because they wore long trousers rather than the knee breeches worn by the nobility.

NAPOLEON BONAPARTE

From 1795-99, the Directory became increasingly dependent on a brilliant young officer from Corsica, named Napoleon Bonaparte (1769-1821). In 1799, Napoleon seized power and made himself First Consul (effectively a dictator). In 1804, he crowned himself Emperor Napoleon I.

The Coronation of Napoleon I (1804) by the French painter Ingres

In many ways Napoleon was an enlightened reformer. He introduced many innovations which shaped modern France. The country was divided into departments, and a new network of roads was built. He introduced schools throughout France, simplified the tax system and set out French law in the *Code Napoléon*.

First edition of the *Code Napoléon* (1804)

Napoleon was also very ambitious. He wanted to create an empire, with himself at its head. By 1812, after a series of brilliant victories, much of Europe was under his control. Francis II of Austria

Napoleon's empire, 1810

was forced to give up his title as Holy Roman Emperor and the German states were reorganized. Napoleon installed his relatives as rulers of Spain, Italy and Westphalia (in western Germany). The subjects in these countries had to pay taxes to France and obey French laws.

In 1812, Napoleon's fortunes changed with a disastrous invasion of Russia. 600,000 French soldiers marched on Moscow but, in the face of fierce Russian opposition, were forced to turn back. It was mid-winter and only 30,000 men survived the retreat in sub-zero temperatures. In 1814, after a series of victories by Austrian, British, Prussian and Russian forces, Napoleon was captured. He was exiled to Elba, an island off the west coast of Italy, but he escaped a year later, returning triumphantly to France. He was finally defeated in 1815, at the Battle of Waterloo (in Belgium) and was exiled to St. Helena (in the Atlantic Ocean), where he died in 1821. The monarchy was restored and Louis XVI's brother was crowned Louis XVIII.

At a meeting in Vienna, in 1815, the rulers of Europe tried to return all European lands to their previous rulers. They defended the authority of kings as the highest authority in the state.

NATIONALISM

The French Revolution spread the idea that people had rights with which governments should not interfere. In many states, this belief became linked with nationalism (the desire for independence from foreign rule) and struggles for independence soon broke out all over the continent.

The Turkish Ottoman empire lost much of its control in Europe. It was forced to grant independence to Greece (1829), Romania, Serbia and Montenegro (all in 1878) and to give Bulgaria a limited form of self-government (1878).

Uprisings in the Hapsburg empire led to self-government for Hungary in 1867. The king of Austria was also crowned king of Hungary and the empire was renamed the Austro-Hungarian Empire.

In Italy and Germany, each made up of separate states, nationalist movements emerged which aimed at creating single nation states. These movements sprang from the ambitions of certain states, namely Piedmont (in Italy) and Prussia (in Germany), but they also sparked off popular nationalist feelings. By 1870, Italy was united. The following year, the Prussian king became emperor of a united Germany.

This is Garibaldi, an Italian patriot. He fought against Austria in 1848 and united southern Italy.

This flag was a symbol of Italian unity and it eventually became the flag of the United Italian kingdom.

INDUSTRY AND EMPIRE

Iron machines, like this one for lowering miners down the pit, were a product of the Industrial Revolution.

By the 20th century most European countries had been transformed by an Industrial Revolution. This meant economies based on farming had been replaced by ones dominated by manufacturing and the use of new machinery. The process began in Britain where, in the first half of the 18th century, great technological progress was made. During the 19th century, it spread to Belgium, France, Germany and Italy.

STEAM POWER

The introduction of steam power was one of the key factors of the Industrial Revolution. Until the 18th century, work either had to be done by hand or by machines powered by animals, water or wind, none of which was very efficient. Steam power enabled inventors to build machines that could work a thousand times as fast as workers using their hands.

One of the first steam-powered machines was a simple pump, invented in 1698 in England by Thomas Savery, and improved by Thomas Newcomen. But it was not until the 1760s that the inventor James Watt built a steam engine that could power a range of machinery. By 1800, over 500 of Watt's engines were being used in Britain.

In the 19th century, the use of steam power spread through Europe, and inventors in Belgium, Germany and northern Italy soon developed their own models. Progress in France, however, was slowed down by the Napoleonic Wars (see page 27).

How Newcomen's steam engine worked:

1 The piston is drawn to the top of the cylinder by a weight on the other side of the rocking beam.

2 Steam from below fills the cylinder.

3 A jet of cold water cools the steam which condenses (turns into water).

4 Water takes up less room than steam, so the piston is forced down to fill the vacuum that is created.

5 The pump rod is forced up and the cycle starts again.

THE BRITISH TEXTILE INDUSTRY

Since the 16th century, the production of cloth had been one of Britain's biggest trades. Until the 1770s, it was run by self-employed craftsmen and women, working from their homes. During the 18th century, however, improvements were made to spinning and weaving machines which meant that better quality cloth could be produced more quickly. In 1764, James Hargreaves invented a machine which could spin up to eight threads at a time, where early machines could only spin one. But the new machines were expensive and many spinners and weavers could not afford them. By the 1780s, machines powered by water and steam were being produced.

James Hargreaves' spinning machine (1764), nicknamed the *Spinning Jenny*

This meant that work had to be done in a factory, at the source of power, and that skilled spinners and weavers were themselves becoming dispensable. Within a century, the cloth trade had turned from a "cottage" industry into a massive factory-based one.

This is a Newcomen steam engine which was used to pump water out of flooded coal mines. The picture has been cut away, so you can see inside it.

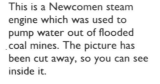

Rocking beam

Pump rod

Piston

Cylinder

Steam chamber

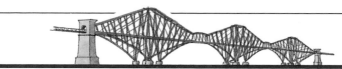

TRANSPORTATION

As industry grew, industrialists needed a new and better way of transporting the greater number of goods being produced. In Britain, a network of canals and roads spread across the country. Building techniques improved, as iron, and eventually steel, replaced wood and stone in the construction of bridges and ships. The greatest revolution, however, came with the invention of the steam train in 1804 by Richard Trevithick. In 1825, the first permanent public railway opened, linking the city of Darlington with the port of Stockton (in northeast England). Soon a vast rail network had sprung up all over Europe and in European colonies.

CHANGING LIVES

What happened in the textile industry in Britain was repeated all over Europe. Self-employed craftsmen and small farmers who could not afford new machinery were forced to find work in factories. This led to a massive shift of population, as people moved from small village communities in the countryside to towns and cities.

Factory workers, including children, were often forced to work long hours for very low pay. Some workers banded together to try to persuade governments and employers to improve working conditions. Eventually organized groups grew up, called trade unions.

Unemployed factory workers waiting for a meal at a charity kitchen

As the 19th century progressed, trade unions became more and more powerful and more political. By the 20th century, many of them had become linked with a political movement called socialism. Socialists argued that governments had a responsibility to protect workers through law, and to share wealth more equally between the rich and the poor .

The steam engine, *The Locomotion*, pulls the first passenger train to Darlington.

OVERSEAS EMPIRES

After the discovery of the New World, many Europeans saw foreign empires as a means of gaining wealth, or simply a new way of life. Portugal, Spain, France and Britain set up trading posts in the Americas, Africa and India. These grew into permanent settlements. They were initially inhabited by traders and governed by trading companies, but governments soon began to rule more directly in many places and to claim great areas of territory. They often lacked the troops to occupy this new land and could hardly do more than hold a few strongpoints. But the control of land became a symbol of power and prestige and often led to rivalries between European powers.

Colonial Africa, 1914

French
British
German
Portuguese
Belgian
Spanish
Italian

AFRICA COLONIZED

At the beginning of the 19th century, central Africa was virtually unknown to Europeans. But, between 1877 and 1914, almost the entire continent was divided up between the European powers. This happened so fast that it is called the Scramble for Africa. There were many reasons for it. The Industrial Revolution encouraged Europeans to find new sources of raw materials and new markets for their goods. The spread of nationalism and the emergence of new nations reduced the scope for expansion in Europe. So, to gain the prestige of an empire, rulers had to look beyond Europe's borders. This was especially important for the newly established nation states of Italy and Germany.

BREAKING FREE

Colonies in which the majority of the population was made up of settlers from the colonial power were the first to demand and achieve independence. In the 18th century, colonists in North America broke away from Britain, and Spain and Portugal lost control in South and Central America. During the 19th century, Britain granted self-government to Australia, New Zealand, Canada and South Africa. After the Second World War, however, the entire colonial system crumbled and, by the 1960s, virtually all European colonies had been granted independence.

This statue of George III was toppled by the citizens of New York in 1776, in protest against British rule.

THE FIRST WORLD WAR

War broke out in Europe in the summer of 1914. On both sides, people thought it would be "all over by Christmas", as the politicians had promised. But it lasted four years, killing more than 10 million people. By 1918, Europe had been politically, economically and socially transformed.

The war is described as the First World War because fighting spread to countries outside Europe, particularly to the colonies of the European powers.

After the war, memorials like this one were built to the dead.

THE BACKGROUND TO WAR

At the beginning of the 20th century, there was much tension between the great powers. France and Russia feared the growing military strength of Germany, and Germany feared being surrounded by hostile powers. Russia and Austria-Hungary disagreed about who should have control in the Balkans. Competition for colonies abroad had also led to bitter rivalries (see page 29).

Against this background of distrust, rival alliances developed. On one side, France, Britain and Russia formed an alliance called the Entente. Opposing them was the alliance between Germany and Austria-Hungary.

The alliance system was meant to make countries feel safer. But instead it created an atmosphere in which a minor dispute between two countries could spark off a general explosion. The spark which set off the First World War came from the Balkans.

An area of political rivalry, the Balkans was (and still is) one of Europe's troublespots. Russia, Turkey and Austria-Hungary all

Archduke Franz Ferdinand in Sarajevo on the day he was assassinated

had empires in the area. Nationalist movements had emerged in the 19th century, led by the independent Balkan state of Serbia. This led to conflict, as small states fought for independence from the empires that ruled them.

On June 28, 1914, the heir to the Austro-Hungarian empire, Archduke Franz Ferdinand, was assassinated by a Serbian nationalist in the Austro-Hungarian town of Sarajevo (now in Bosnia). Austria-Hungary immediately presented Serbia with a set of demands, as compensation. Serbia refused to follow them and, on July 28, 1914, Austria declared war.

Within weeks, war broke out between the two alliances. Austria-Hungary and Germany, known as the Central Powers, were later joined by Turkey (1914) and Bulgaria (1915). The Entente powers, known as the Allies, were joined by Italy (1915), Greece (1915), Portugal (1916), Romania (1917) and the USA (1917).

A British poster encouraging young men to join the army

YOUR KING & COUNTRY NEED YOU

A CHIP OF THE OLD BLOCK

TO MAINTAIN THE HONOUR AND GLORY OF THE BRITISH EMPIRE

Trenches were wet and muddy for most of the year. Many men were crippled by a disease called trench foot, caused by the wet conditions.

THE COURSE OF THE WAR

The Germans had the largest army, and were confident that they could win the war within months. Their plan was to defeat France and Britain in the west, before the Russians had had a chance to organize their forces in the east. But their plans failed. On the Western front, a stalemate arose. Both sides dug themselves into fortified ditches, called trenches. Soldiers trying to advance faced deadly fire from machine guns and cannons, from an enemy they could not even see. Territory was gained and

British troops in the trenches, 1916

The area between enemy trenches was called "no man's land".

Trenches were reinforced with wooden planks.

Sand bags

lost, little by little, in bloody battles that cost thousands of lives. At one battle alone, the Battle of the Somme (from July 1-November 19, 1916), 1,043,896 casualties (dead and wounded) were recorded. On the Eastern front, where the Germans fought the Russians, a similar situation arose. But after heavy losses on both sides, the Russians finally withdrew from the war in 1917.

The deadlock in the west began to break when, in April 1917, the USA entered the war on the Allied side. The arrival of fit men and new fire power gave the Allies the advantage they needed. On November 11, 1918, the Germans called for an armistice (a halt in the fighting) to allow for peace talks.

Europe 1914-18

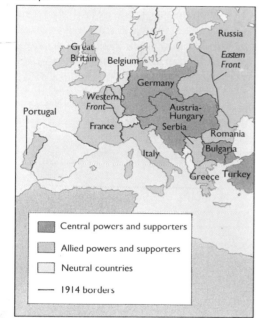

- Central powers and supporters
- Allied powers and supporters
- Neutral countries
- 1914 borders

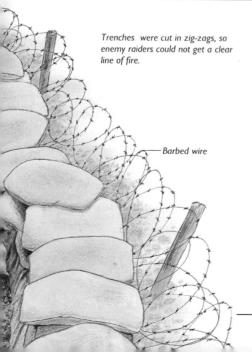

Trenches were cut in zig-zags, so enemy raiders could not get a clear line of fire.

— Barbed wire

WOMEN AT WAR

A woman working at a weapons factory

Women played a vital role in the war. With so many men at the front, women had to take over traditionally male jobs in factories. This challenged the widely held idea that women should not work outside the home. After the war, it became more acceptable for women to seek employment in industry and government. In many countries, women's contribution to the war effort helped them win the right to vote.

PEACEMAKING AND THE NEW EUROPE

Four years of fighting left Europe in a state of confusion. The Austro-Hungarian and German empires fell and the Ottoman empire lost all but a corner of its European territory. The Russian empire, weakened by the war, was toppled and replaced by a communist government. Peace talks, held at Versailles, outside Paris, had to find a way to reconstruct European nations from the wreckage of the old empires. As the USA had played such a major role in ending the war, the US president, Woodrow Wilson, had great influence at the peace talks.

Woodrow Wilson (1856-1924)

Wilson wanted to abandon the old European system of the balance of power (see page 24). Instead he wanted a Europe made up of small states based on national groups (people who spoke the same language and shared a common culture). Peace treaties were drawn up which gave independence to states previously ruled by large empires.

Wilson's new Europe created as many problems as it solved. National groups were not always found in neat blocks around which frontiers could be drawn, so many of the new states contained unhappy minorities. This has caused tensions throughout the 20th century.

Several of the new states were sandwiched between Germany and Russia.

Although both had been weakened by the war, it was not long before they were strong enough to dominate the weaker countries that surrounded them.

Germany was dealt with by the Treaty of Versailles, which reflected Allied hatred of the Germans. The French went into the peace talks with the slogan: "Germany will pay", to which the British added: "to the last penny". The treaty demanded that Germany pay the Allies huge sums of money and give up large amounts of land. The Germans were forbidden to build up new armed forces or to station troops in the Rhineland. Also, much against their will, they were forced to admit guilt for the war. All this was bitterly resented by the Germans.

Post-war Europe, 1918

- Land lost by Germany
- Land lost by Austria-Hungary
- Land lost by the Ottoman Empire
- Land lost by Russia
- Land lost by Bulgaria
- FINLAND   New nation state

MARX, LENIN AND STALIN

Karl Marx (1818-83)

For much of the 20th century, European politics has been deeply affected by an ideology known as communism. Communism is a set of political beliefs based on the theories of Karl Marx, a German-born philosopher. Marx predicted that, as a result of the industrial revolution, the factory workers (whom he called the proletariat) would revolt against their bosses. The proletariat would then set up a dictatorship, in which industry and agriculture would be run by the state. People would not be allowed to own land or businesses, or to make money for themselves. Eventually the need for a dictatorship would end and all citizens would live as equals. Each person would be given what they needed from the state. In return all would work for the community.

The uprising Marx predicted never took place, but his ideas were developed by other political thinkers, including a Russian lawyer called Lenin. Lenin argued that the proletariat could not organize a revolution on its own, and that a group of leaders was needed to seize power before the dictatorship of the proletariat could begin.

This is the title page of *The Communist Manifesto* (1848), in which Marx urged workers to unite and revolt.

Lenin addressing a rally in Petrograd, 1917

COMMUNISM COMES TO RUSSIA

In the 19th century, Russia was socially and economically backward compared to the rest of Europe. The country had not experienced an industrial revolution, and the peasants and the few factory workers there were lived in great poverty. The middle class had little political power. By 1900, opposition to the tsar (the emperor) was growing.

The First World War heightened the hardship and suffering in Russia. Thousands lost their homes in the fighting and headed to the cities to work in weapons factories. Food was in short supply, as the war hindered the delivery of crops from the country to the towns.

In protest, hungry and frustrated workers formed committees, called soviets, and organized strikes and marches. In February 1917, these soviets led a series of strikes in the city of Petrograd (now St. Petersburg). The army refused to crush the rebellion, and the tsar was forced to abdicate. This is known as the February Revolution. Power in Russia was then taken by a provisional government, made up of middle-class reformers. But it was unable to assert its control over the Petrograd soviet, which emerged as an alternative government, giving orders to other soviets in Russia.

Lenin saw the situation in Petrograd as a chance to put his beliefs into practice. On the night of October 24, 1917, he and his supporters (known as Bolsheviks) stormed the Winter Palace and the parliament building, forcing the provisional government to hand over power. This is known as the October Revolution.

The Communist Party in Russia has always tried to portray this event as a mass uprising by the workers. But it was in fact a well-planned seizure of

This painting by the Russian communist artist Sokolov-Skalya portrays the Communist Party view of the storming of the Winter Palace.

power carried out by relatively few people. In 1927, Sergei Eisenstein, a Russian director, was commissioned by the Party to make a film about the revolution. The number of actors he employed was greater than the number of people involved in the revolution itself.

Once in power, Lenin got rid of anyone who opposed him, including the tsar and his family, who were executed without trial. Although much land and industry were taken over by the state, Marx's idea of a dictatorship by the proletariat never happened. Power remained in the hands of Lenin and his Bolshevik supporters.

Posters were a useful way to get across the communist message. This poster says, "As long as the red rifle is in the peasant's hands, nobody will dare threaten your freedom".

In December 1922, Lenin declared Russia and its territories the Union of Soviet Socialist Republics (USSR), also known as the Soviet Union.

STALIN'S SOVIET UNION

When Lenin died in 1924, he was succeeded by Josef Stalin. Stalin introduced reforms which brought more land and industry under state ownership. Through a series of modernizations, he succeeded in turning the USSR into a progressive industrialized nation. But the people paid a heavy price for their country's achievements.

Josef Stalin (1879-1953)

The first step in Stalin's reform plan was the collectivization of agriculture. This meant that the state took all land away from its owners. Peasants were organized to work on state-run farms, which supplied food for government factory workers in the cities. Many of the land-owning peasant farmers bitterly opposed this new policy and refused to work on the new farms. This caused food shortages in the cities. Stalin's response was swift and ruthless. Hundreds of thousands of peasants were rounded up and executed, or exiled to Siberia, a remote and harsh region of the eastern USSR.

During the 1930s, Stalin ruled by fear and terror. He disposed of anyone he believed to be a threat to his position. Between 1934 and 1939, seven million Soviet officials, including senior Communist Party members, industrial managers and high ranking military officers, were arrested in a series of purges. As many as 90% of them were executed or sent to prison camps.

Peasant farmers awaiting deportation from their village, 1930. Some of them made banners protesting against Stalin's treatment of them.

As many as 10 million farmers were forced from their land.

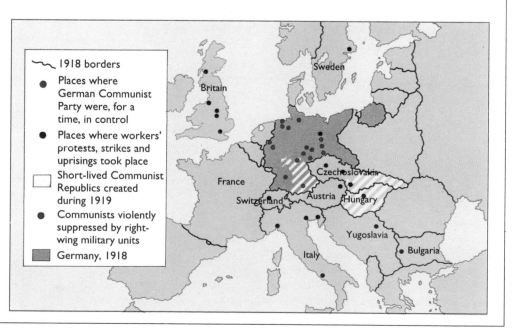

These people were forced to hand over their land and equipment to the collective farms before they were sent away. There are even accounts of troops taking the boots from people's feet and blankets from babies' cradles

This mock tourist poster by Russian exiles portrays Stalin showing visitors the USSR's "pyramids".

INTERNATIONAL COMMUNISM

After the First World War, the governments and privileged classes of Europe feared that communism would spread through the continent. In 1919, the Bolsheviks set up an organization called Comintern to help foreign communist parties organize revolution. Communist parties sprang up all over Europe, and strikes, mutinies and riots were widespread. But only in Germany and Hungary were there attempts at revolution. In Germany, the communists were brutally suppressed. In Hungary, a communist state was set up in 1919, but it survived only four months and was replaced by a military dictatorship.

⌇ 1918 borders

● Places where German Communist Party were, for a time, in control

● Places where workers' protests, strikes and uprisings took place

☐ Short-lived Communist Republics created during 1919

● Communists violently suppressed by right-wing military units

▨ Germany, 1918

THE RISE OF FASCISM

In the aftermath of the First World War, Europe was on the verge of economic collapse. Governments had borrowed vast sums of money to pay for the war and were severely in debt. Poverty was widespread, unemployment was high and many people were starving.

Many states (some of them new nations created by the Treaty of Versailles) introduced democracy for the first time after the war. But, in many places, people felt that their democratic governments could not provide solutions to the problems they faced. They began to look instead to strong leaders who promised more stable and effective government. By 1938, barely a dozen democratic nations were left in Europe and a new non-democratic political ideology, called fascism, had taken root.

In 1922, Mussolini became prime minister. He abolished opposition parties and took away democratic rights. Industry, education, the media, trade unions and even sports were brought under his control.

Today the word fascist is used to describe any ruler who follows Mussolini's policy of authoritarian rule and excessive nationalism.

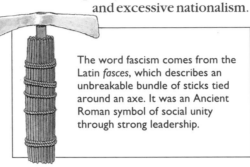

The word fascism comes from the Latin *fasces*, which describes an unbreakable bundle of sticks tied around an axe. It was an Ancient Roman symbol of social unity through strong leadership.

Adolf Hitler (1889-1945)

Opponents were sent to special prisons called concentration camps. In 1934, Hitler named himself *Führer* (German for "leader") and the Nazi regime became a harsh dictatorship.

MUSSOLINI: THE FIRST MODERN FASCIST

The modern fascist movement was founded in Italy in 1919 by Benito Mussolini. Fascists believed that the needs of the nation were more important than individual rights. Fascist states tried to control every aspect of people's lives.

Benito Mussolini (1883-1945)

Mussolini promised to make Italy a powerful military and economic force and he won support from many different social groups. Workers believed fascism would protect them from low wages, while the middle classes saw it as a weapon against communism.

THE RISE OF HITLER

Germany was particularly badly hit by the post-war depression and suffered severe food shortages and high unemployment. In the 1920s, inflation soared. Prices rose so quickly that money became almost worthless. Women had to take sackfuls of money to the shops just to buy a loaf of bread.

Money was so worthless, some German children were allowed to make a kite out of it.

Many Germans blamed the new democratic government. Some workers saw communism as the answer to their problems. But others turned to the National Socialist Party (the Nazis), led by Adolf Hitler, which pledged to recover German power and prestige. The Nazis promised stable government, economic reform and falling unemployment. In 1933, they became the biggest party in the German parliament and Hitler was made Chancellor (head of the government). He passed laws banning opposition parties, trade unions and any other group that threatened his position.

HITLER AS FÜHRER

Hitler delivered the economic recovery he had promised. He introduced schemes which employed thousands of people in jobs, such as road building and slum-clearing. Between 1933 and 1935, unemployment fell from six million to two and a half million.

From 1933-38, annual meetings of the Nazi party were held at Nuremburg, during which military parades and mass rallies took place.

But there was a more sinister side of Nazism. Hitler believed that Germans were a superior people, a "master race". He wanted to unite all German-speaking people and create a Greater Germany, which would become the heart of a New Europe dominated by the Germans.

Hitler sponsored the making of the *Volkswagen Beetle* (the "people's car"), to boost the German car industry and to create jobs.

Hitler's immediate aim as Führer was to "harmonize" Germany. This meant creating a community of pure Germans who shared Nazi beliefs. All newspapers, radio broadcasts and films were put under government control and forced to put across the Nazi message. Schools and universities had to teach subjects from a Nazi point of view. Outside school hours, young people were encouraged to join the Nazi-controlled Hitler Youth (for boys) or the League of Maidens (for girls). A secret police force, called the *Gestapo*, kept watch over people's daily lives, looking for signs of anti-Nazi activities, and punishing all dissenters. People that Hitler believed did not belong to the master race, particularly the Jews, were treated as social outcasts and persecuted. In November 1938, after a German diplomat was killed by a 17 year old Jewish boy in Paris, Hitler launched a campaign of violence against the Jews. On one night alone, thousands of windows of Jewish shops were smashed. The glinting of street

Nazi soldiers enforce a boycott of Jewish shops.

lights on the broken glass has given this event the name *Kristallnacht*, which means "crystal night".

THE COUNTDOWN TO WAR

Hitler wanted to make Germany strong enough to go to war again. So he ignored the restrictions on arms production placed on the country after the First World War. Factories began making war machinery and, in 1935, compulsory military service was introduced. This meant all young men had to join the forces. By 1938, Hitler was ready to begin his plans for a Greater Germany and a New Europe.

In March, German troops marched into Austria. In May, they seized large areas of Czechoslovakia. In September, Hitler signed an agreement with Britain and France, promising to advance no farther. But a month later his troops invaded the rest of Czechoslovakia. Britain and France feared Hitler would overrun central Europe. So they promised to send troops to Greece, Poland and Romania if any of these countries were attacked by Germany.

On August 23, 1939, Germany and the USSR signed the Nazi-Soviet Pact. Hitler and Stalin agreed a secret plan to divide up Poland between them. On September 1, 1939, Hitler invaded Poland and, on September 3, France and Britain declared war on Germany.

The swastika was the symbol of the Nazi Party.

Hundreds of soldiers were employed at rallies to carry Nazi flags.

THE SECOND WORLD WAR

French soldiers surrendering to the Germans

From the spring of 1940, Hitler's troops swept through Europe. Between April and June, they invaded Norway, Denmark, Belgium, Holland and France. The French, British and Belgian forces (known as the Allies) were forced to retreat into northern France. In May 1940, they were evacuated to Britain from the port of Dunkirk. Then Hitler turned his attention to Britain. In the summer of 1940, the *Luftwaffe* (the German air force) began a series of attacks against Britain and the RAF (the British air force), possibly in preparation for invasion. This is known as the Battle of Britain. By December, the *Luftwaffe* was defeated and the threat of invasion lifted.

In 1941, Hitler sent his forces to southeast Europe, where his troops won decisive victories in Greece and Yugoslavia. In North Africa, German troops with their Italian allies (together known as the Axis powers) advanced into Allied territory in Egypt.

On June 22, 1941, Hitler mounted an attack on the Soviet Union, codenamed "Operation Barbarossa". The USSR had large areas of farmland and other resources which Hitler wanted for Germany. By December, Nazi troops had occupied the western provinces of the USSR and were still heading east. Despite enormous losses, however, the Soviet army did not surrender.

EUROPE UNDER THE NAZIS

Nazi motorcyclists followed planes and tanks into conquered territory.

The Nazis took over industries and farms in the countries they occupied, and local workers were sent to Germany to work in factories. People often starved because crops were sent to Germany too. Most bitterly resented Nazi rule, but accepted it out of fear. A minority, known as the Resistance, actively opposed the occupation, sometimes using terrorist tactics. Nazi response to the Resistance was often brutal. In one incident, an entire French village was wiped out, in retaliation for a Resistance attack on a train.

An air battle (nicknamed a dog-fight) during the Battle of Britain, 1940.

The German Messerschmitt 109E, nicknamed "Emil" by the Germans

Machine guns in wings and nose

British identification marks

THE "FINAL SOLUTION"

Hitler proposed the extermination of the entire Jewish race in Europe as the "final solution" to what he saw as the Jewish problem. Jews were frequently beaten, shot, burned and starved to death. Many millions were rounded up and sent to death camps, where they were killed in gas chambers. Between 1941 and 1945, as many as six million Jews were killed.

The gas chambers were also used for other members of society that Hitler considered impure or dangerous. These included gypsies, homosexuals, the clergy and the disabled. Historians believe that another six million people may have been murdered.

Europe under Hitler, 1939-41

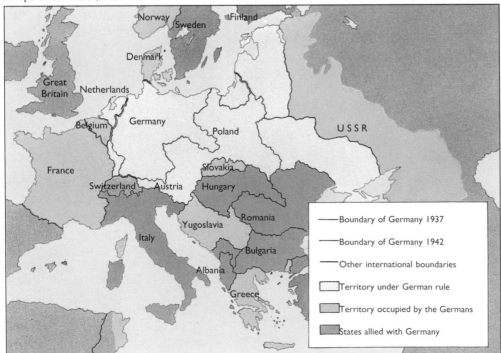

— Boundary of Germany 1937

— Boundary of Germany 1942

— Other international boundaries

Territory under German rule

Territory occupied by the Germans

States allied with Germany

German identification marks

British Vickers Supermarine Spitfire
IA single-seater fighter

A pilot bails out of his
burning plane.

Machine guns in
the wings fired out
of gun holes.

WAR IN THE PACIFIC

On December 7, 1941, the Japanese bombed Pearl Harbor, a US naval base in Hawaii, as part of their plan to control the Pacific. The USA and Britain declared war on Japan and three days later, Germany and Italy (Japan's allies) declared war on the USA. The Japanese occupied many countries in the Far East, some of them European colonies. Although the Allies steadily reclaimed their territory, the Japanese resisted fiercely. In August 1945, the war came to an abrupt end when the Americans dropped two atomic bombs on the Japanese cities of Hiroshima and Nagasaki. Against weapons with such destructive power, the Japanese had no choice but to surrender.

An atomic bomb
explodes over the city of
Hiroshima.

THE ALLIED COUNTER-OFFENSIVE

In 1942, the tide began to turn. The German advance in Russia was slowed down by the harsh winter of 1941-42, as their army was ill-equipped to deal with sub-zero temperatures. This gave the Soviet army time to regroup. In November 1942, Soviet troops launched a counterattack at Stalingrad (now Volgagrad) where the German army was finally defeated in February 1943.

A German tank stuck in
frozen mud in Russia.

The Soviet army then began slowly to expel the Germans from the USSR.

In the meantime, the western Allies were winning important battles in North Africa and the Mediterranean. In October 1942, the British won a decisive victory at the Battle of El Alamein in Egypt. With the help of the Americans, who had joined the war in 1941, the Allies forced the Axis powers to retreat from North Africa. The joint Anglo-American forces then crossed the Mediterranean and invaded Italy. In September 1943, Italy surrendered.

On June 6, 1944, codenamed D-Day, an Anglo-American force landed on the beaches of Normandy in northern France. By December, France was liberated, and the Germans were in retreat. At the same time, the Soviet army was advancing westward, liberating eastern Europe. On April 24, 1945, Soviet troops entered Berlin. On April 25, Allied forces from east and west linked up on the River Elbe. Five days later, Adolf Hitler

committed suicide in his underground Berlin headquarters. Within a few weeks, Germany surrendered unconditionally and the war in Europe was over.

Soviet troops flying the Soviet flag over Berlin

THE COLD WAR: EUROPE DIVIDED

The Soviet view of the West: a world of luxuries with five million unemployed.

On April 24, 1945, as Berlin fell to the Allies, American and Soviet troops met and shook hands at Torgue, on the River Elbe. But this unity did not extend to the Allied leaders. As the war came to an end, a state of hostility grew up between the democratic governments of Western Europe and the communist governments of Eastern Europe. For nearly fifty years, East and West fought a battle of propaganda and threats, which is known as the Cold War.

US and Soviet troops shake hands at Torgue.

THE "IRON CURTAIN" DESCENDS

In March 1946, Winston Churchill (the former British prime minister) described the post-war east/west divide as an "iron curtain" which had descended over the continent.

Europe divided, 1946

Communist countries linked to the USSR	Other communist countries
	— The Iron Curtain

Poland
Czechoslovakia
Hungary
Romania
Yugoslavia
Bulgaria
Albania
USSR

The division arose out of the post-war peace settlements. Stalin demanded that former Axis territory be given to the USSR, as compensation for the enormous Soviet losses during the war. The British and the Americans agreed. In return, Stalin promised to withdraw his troops from the Eastern European countries they had liberated from the Nazis, and to allow free elections.

But Stalin did not call his troops home. It soon became clear that the new Eastern European governments could not survive without toeing the Moscow line. A zone of Soviet-controlled countries (the Soviet bloc) was created between the USSR and the rest of Western Europe.

TIT-FOR-TAT

The first "battle" of the Cold War was over money. The US government offered Europe a massive aid package of over $13 billion, known as the Marshall Plan. The aid was given to reduce poverty and to build up western capitalist economies, which would, at the same time, provide the US with markets in which to sell their goods. The Soviets condemned the Marshall Plan as a bribe and introduced their own aid package known as COMECON, to help rebuild Eastern Europe. But they did not have the funds to help the East to the extent that the United States could help countries in the West.

In 1949, reacting to what they saw as a military threat from the USSR and the Soviet bloc, the western allies (including the USA) formed a military alliance, the North Atlantic Treaty Organization (NATO). The members of NATO promised to defend each other if any one of them were attacked. In 1955, the USSR responded by creating the Warsaw Pact, a similar agreement signed by all Soviet bloc countries.

DIVIDED GERMANY

After the war, Germany was divided into four zones, under the control of Britain, France, the USA and the Soviet Union. The capital, Berlin, which fell in the Soviet sector, was divided up between the Allies in the same way. This was meant to be only a temporary arrangement.

A stretch of the Berlin Wall in the middle of the city

Soviet tank

Soviet soldiers

The Brandenburg Gate was built in 1789-93, to celebrate Prussian military victories. In 1961, it became a symbol of loss of freedom, as people were stopped from passing through it.

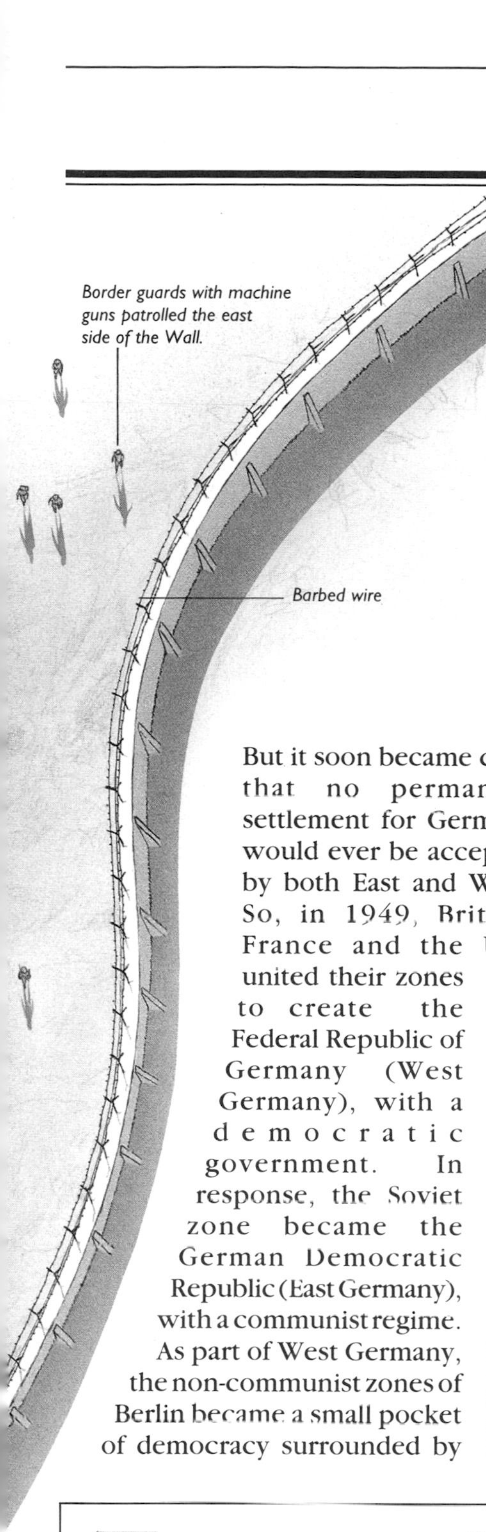

Border guards with machine guns patrolled the east side of the Wall.

Barbed wire

Berlin divided, 1949

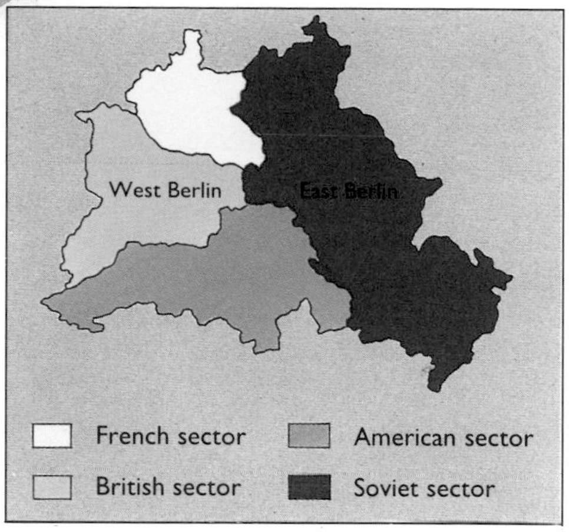

West Berlin

East Berlin

	French sector		American sector
	British sector		Soviet sector

The iron curtain split the economic, social and political life of Europe in two. In Western Europe, people enjoyed more freedom and a steady rise in their standard of living. By contrast, in the USSR and Eastern Europe, people's lives were controlled by the state. No one could speak or write freely, because anything seen as a threat to communism was banned. People were subjected to a constant stream of propaganda and those who opposed the state were sent to prison.

This Soviet poster (1961) proclaims that, "The banner of the Revolution will not fade with time!"

ЗНАМЯ РЕВОЛЮЦИИ НЕ ПОМЕРКНЕТ В ВЕКАХ!

But it soon became clear that no permanent settlement for Germany would ever be accepted by both East and West. So, in 1949, Britain, France and the USA united their zones to create the Federal Republic of Germany (West Germany), with a democratic government. In response, the Soviet zone became the German Democratic Republic (East Germany), with a communist regime. As part of West Germany, the non-communist zones of Berlin became a small pocket of democracy surrounded by communist East Germany. People from the East soon began pouring into West Berlin to escape the communist regime. West Berlin seemed to many to be a better place to live. People were less poor because of Marshall Aid, and had more freedom because of democracy. In 1961, to stop the flood of escapees, the communist authorities built a wall sealing off East from West Berlin. This left families and friends divided. Until 1989, when it was pulled down, many East Germans risked their lives trying to get across the Wall. Those that were seen were shot by guards.

An East German soldier jumps a coil of barbed wire into the West before the Wall is completed.

After Brezhnev became Soviet leader in the 1960s, communism began to fail economically. His leadership is known as the Period of Stagnation because no reforms were made. The failure of communism to solve economic problems contributed to the break up of the Soviet bloc in the 1990s.

US V USSR

Although the dividing line between East and West was a European one, the Cold War was really a struggle between the USSR and the USA.

Throughout the Cold War, the USA and the USSR competed to bring nations from all over the world into their own political camps. They often supplied arms and money to opposing sides in overseas conflicts, such as the Korean and Vietnam wars. Although hostilities never broke out directly between the two sides, for over 30 years there was a real threat of nuclear war. Both sides developed missiles that were capable of massive destruction.

This diagram shows how nuclear capability increased from 1960-69.

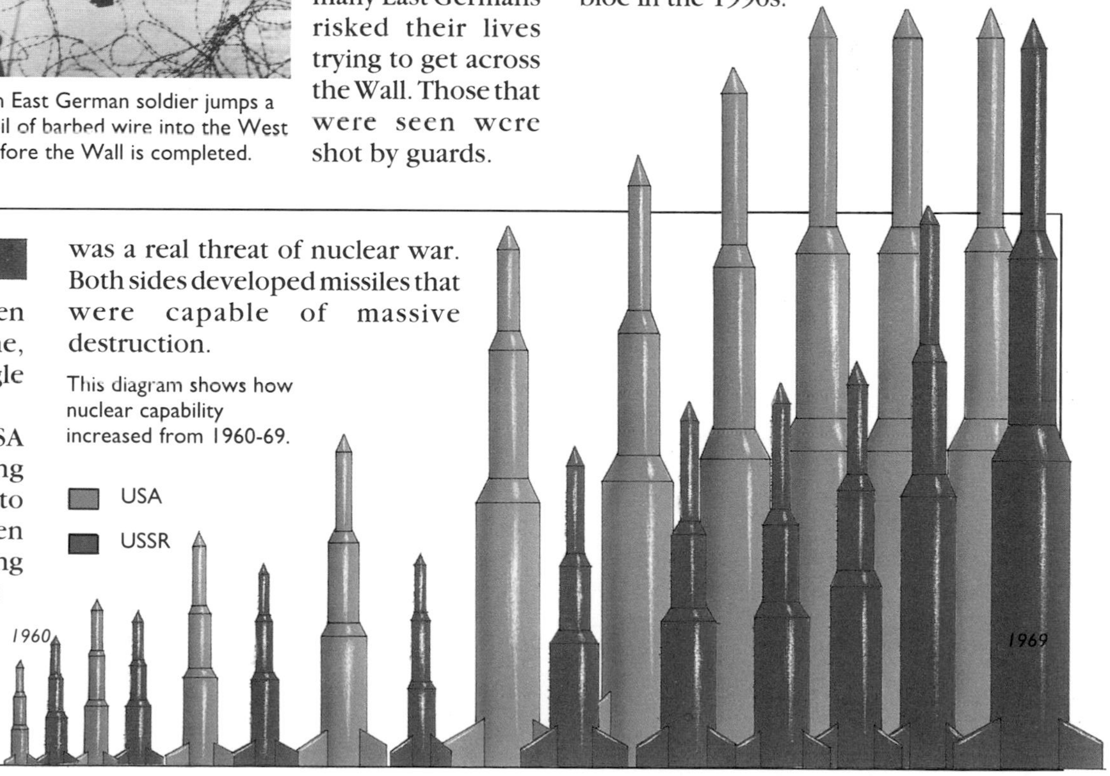

USA

USSR

1960

1969

The European Community flag

Throughout history, the nations of Europe have been more or less constantly at war with each other. But after two bloody world wars, many Europeans felt it was time to find a way to live without conflict. The wars had killed millions and shattered Europe's economies. Many people began to believe that Europe could only survive economically and militarily by acting as a single unit, rather than as individual states.

FIRST STEPS

The first step to achieving this unity was made when France, Germany, Belgium, Luxembourg, the Netherlands and Italy signed the Treaty of Paris in 1951. The treaty set up the European Coal and Steel Community (ECSC), which prevented any member state (nation which had signed the treaty) from using these industries to prepare for war.

In 1957, the same countries signed the Treaty of Rome, which set up the European Economic Community (EEC). The EEC aimed to make European trade easier and cheaper, by reducing the taxes that had to be paid when goods were transported between member states. At the same time, Euratom, the European Atomic Energy Community, was created. This encouraged joint nuclear energy projects and set up a committee which could inspect the nuclear power sites of the members.

The ECSC, the EEC and Euratom together make up what today is called the European Community (EC). Since the 1950s, however, the Community has doubled the number of member states and become more and more powerful. It is now a massive organization, representing over 350 million people, with its own Parliament, its own laws and its own flag.

The Community is run by four main institutions: the European Commission, the European Parliament, the Council of Ministers and the Court of Justice.

THE COMMISSION

The Commission meets in Brussels, in Belgium, to consider proposals for new Community laws. It is made up of one or more representatives from each member state. Although commissioners are appointed by the governments of each member state, their role is to act only in the interests of the Community as a whole. The Commission itself answers to the European Parliament and sends its proposals to the Parliament to be debated. The Commission then adjusts them to take into account Parliament's opinion. The proposals are then passed to the Council of Ministers, which decides whether or not they should become law.

The Commission also has to make sure that Community rules are kept. It is able to fine individuals or companies that break EC rules and can bring member states before the Court of Justice.

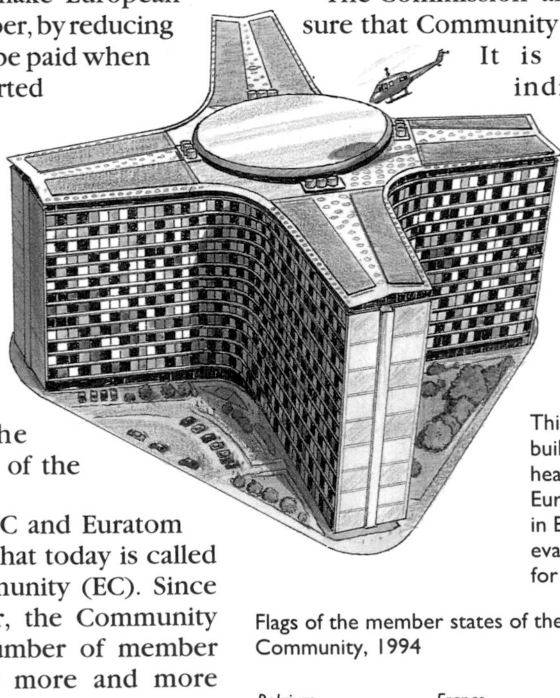

This is the Berlaymont building, the former headquarters of the European Commission in Brussels. It was evacuated in the 1990s for safety reasons.

THE EUROPEAN PARLIAMENT

There are over 500 members of the European Parliament, known as MEPs or "Euro MPs". MEPs are elected every five years by the people of the countries they represent.

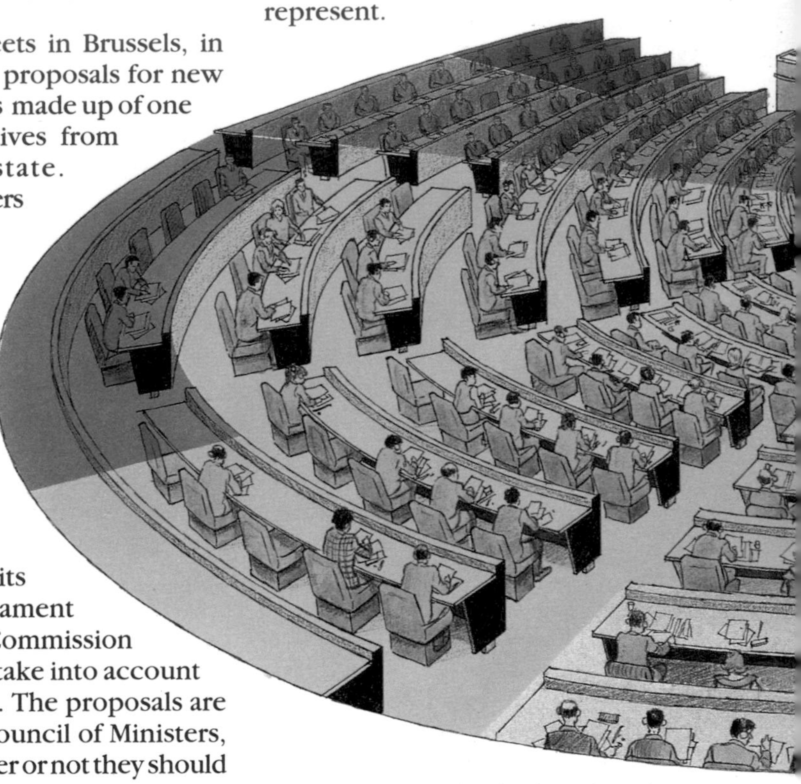

This diagram shows the chamber where the European Parliament meets, in Strasbourg, eastern France.

The number of MEPs each country elects depends on the size of its population (see chart, shown on right).

MEPs discuss and comment on the policies and laws proposed by the Commission. They suggest changes and then return the proposals to the Commission. Some proposals have to go through Parliament a second time, before they can be sent to the Council of Ministers. MEPs also draw Parliament's attention to the problems of the people in the countries they represent.

The European Parliament has 19 permanent committees made up of MEPs from different political groups. They recommend amendments to Commission proposals on a wide range of issues, from human rights to transport.

Flags of the member states of the European Community, 1994

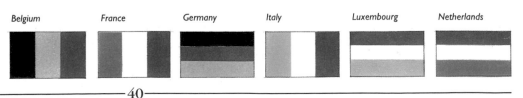

| Belgium | France | Germany | Italy | Luxembourg | Netherlands |

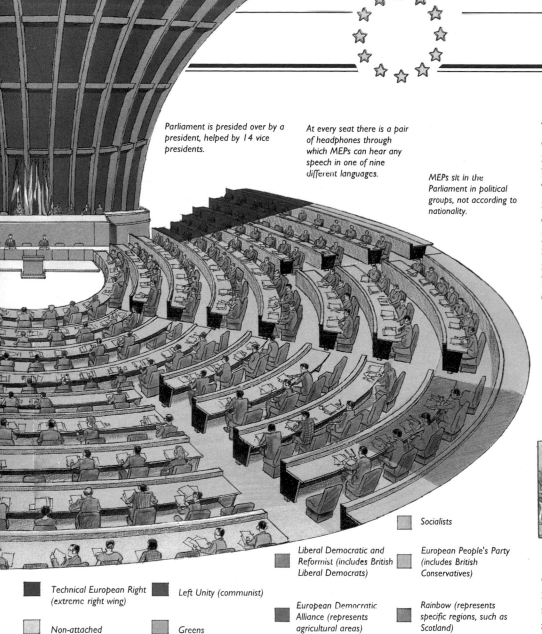

Parliament is presided over by a president, helped by 14 vice presidents.

At every seat there is a pair of headphones through which MEPs can hear any speech in one of nine different languages.

MEPs sit in the Parliament in political groups, not according to nationality.

Socialists

Liberal Democratic and Reformist (includes British Liberal Democrats)

European People's Party (includes British Conservatives)

Technical European Right (extreme right wing)

Left Unity (communist)

European Democratic Alliance (represents agricultural areas)

Rainbow (represents specific regions, such as Scotland)

Non-attached

Greens

This chart gives you more facts and figures about each member state.

Member state	Year joined EC	No. of MEPS (from June 1994)	No. of votes in Council	Population
Belgium	Founder member	25	5	9,947,800
France	Founder member	87	10	56,304,000
Germany	Founder member	99	10	80,600,000
Italy	Founder member	87	10	57,576,400
Luxembourg	Founder member	6	2	378,400
Netherlands	Founder member	31	5	14,891,900
United Kingdom	1973	87	10	57,326,600
Ireland	1973	15	3	3,498,800
Denmark	1973	16	3	5,135,400
Greece	1981	25	5	10,046,000
Spain	1986	64	8	38,924,500
Portugal	1986	25	5	10,335,200
Austria	1995	21	3	7,860,000
Finland	1995	16	3	5,050,000
Sweden	1995	22	4	8,770,000

Denmark   Ireland   United Kingdom   Greece   Portugal   Spain

THE COUNCIL OF MINISTERS

The Council of Ministers makes the final decisions on the Commission's proposals for new Community law, after they have been passed by the European Parliament. The Council is made up of government ministers from each member state. If, for example, the meeting is about farming policy, agriculture ministers attend, or if it is about pollution, environment ministers. Some proposals can only become law if there is a unanimous vote (i.e. if all the ministers agree to it). Other proposals can become law when only a majority of ministers agrees to it. This is called qualified majority voting (QMV).

The number of votes ministers have depends mainly on the population of their nation (see chart).

A meeting of the Council of Ministers

Some Commissioners want the Council of Ministers to adopt majority voting more often. They believe that it would speed up the decision-making process and give the Community more power over individual member states. But ministers from some countries are opposed to majority voting. They see it as undemocratic, because it allows the EC to impose laws on national governments without their agreement.

In 1975, the European Council was established. This brings together the President of the European Commission and the heads of each member state. It meets twice a year, or more if necessary, to discuss general Community affairs and policies. Usually foreign ministers are also invited to attend.

THE COURT OF JUSTICE

One judge from each member state is appointed to sit on the European Court of Justice, which is situated in Luxembourg. The Court is responsible for settling arguments about the meaning of Community laws and for ensuring that the laws are kept.

LIVING IN THE EC

Member states issue passports which grant EC citizenship as well as nationality.

The EC, or European Community, affects the lives of all its citizens in every member state. As well as making important political decisions which governments have to follow, the EC also introduces many laws on more everyday matters.

The imaginary European town below shows how people's lives are affected by the European Community.

ECONOMIC POLICY

One of the first aims of the EC was to create a single market. In a single market, goods can pass between countries without taxes being paid. By the end of 1992, all EC countries had abolished import and export duties (taxes on goods entering and leaving each country). This means that when selling cars in Germany, for example, a German car maker has no advantage over a French car maker. Because of this, goods will eventually become cheaper under the single market, as they will be produced where they can be made most efficiently.

Many member states in the EC want to take the single market a step further and are working for a single European currency, known as the *ecu*. They believe the ecu would make Europe's economy more stable, and would help business and industry. New European coins and paper money would be issued by a European bank, and national governments would not be able to control their own currency. But not all member states are happy with this idea. Some people are worried that it will lead to a loss of national identity, giving the Community too much control over national economic policy.

In supermarkets, all food labels have to carry extensive information about ingredients. Products from all over the Community are easily available.

Schools run special EC language courses for pupils of all ages.

A young person on an EC training placement gets on-the-job experience of a skilled craft.

An EC visitor from another member state takes money out of an automatic money dispenser.

EC health standards are enforced in restaurant kitchens.

EC FARMING

In the 1957 Treaty of Rome (see page 40), the basis of a common agricultural policy (CAP) was drawn up. CAP aimed to ensure that farms produced enough food, so that member states did not have buy products from non-EC countries. Farmers were promised a fair standard of living, and reasonable prices were guaranteed for their products.

The EC spends up to 60% of its total budget on CAP. In many ways, it has been successful. The risk of unemployment for farmers has been reduced. Farms have become more efficient, and the EC needs to import only sweet corn and tropical crops, such as bananas, from non-EC countries.

There are, however, criticisms of CAP. Industrial countries, such as Britain, resent the fact that so much money is spent on farmers. Poorer non-EC countries that used to export their farming goods to Europe have lost an important market. The EC buys produce that farmers cannot sell (surpluses) and this leads to the so-called food mountains and lakes. Storing and disposing of surpluses is very expensive. Many feel that much more should be done to send them to developing countries instead.

A UNITED STATES OF EUROPE?

There is a phrase in the Treaty of Rome which commits all members states to seeking an "ever closer union". People disagree about just what this means.

There are some who want Europe to become a federation: a collection of states ruled by one central authority (like, for example, the USA). This would mean that national governments would have to give up many of their law-making powers and hand them over to the European Community. Other people, known as "Euro-sceptics", are against handing over too many powers to the EC. They argue that each EC nation should remain as independent as possible.

Many politicians take a middle road. They do not want the EC to have complete political control, but believe that some decisions can be made only by the Community. For example, many think that anti-pollution laws could be passed only by the EC. National governments would find it politically very difficult to introduce environmental laws which would cost their industries a great deal of money and make them less profitable.

INTO THE FUTURE

In February 1992, the European Council met in the Dutch town of Maastricht and drew up a new treaty. The Treaty of Maastricht brought political and economic union nearer, which pleased pro-federalist states, such as France and Germany. For member states that were uneasy about further union, such as Britain and Denmark, the treaty offered some "opt-out" clauses.

The Maastricht Treaty paved the way for many new European projects, such as a European police force and a European army. But the future of the European Community is uncertain. With the opening up of Eastern Europe, some people feel that a purely western European Community is too limited and would make economic recovery more difficult for the East. Others think that there is so much disagreement already that any further union will be impossible. But there are also those who see European union as the great hope for the future, ensuring peace and cooperation between all Europeans.

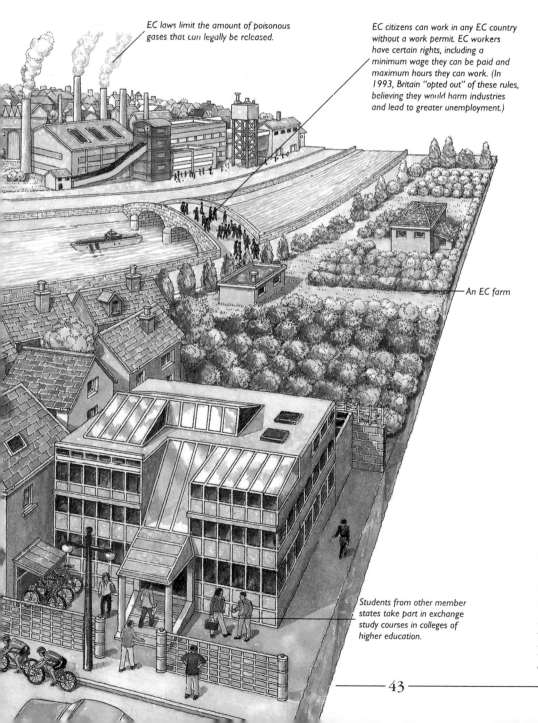

EC laws limit the amount of poisonous gases that can legally be released.

EC citizens can work in any EC country without a work permit. EC workers have certain rights, including a minimum wage they can be paid and maximum hours they can work. (In 1993, Britain "opted out" of these rules, believing they would harm industries and lead to greater unemployment.)

An EC farm

Students from other member states take part in exchange study courses in colleges of higher education.

THE BREAK-UP OF THE SOVIET BLOC

When Mikhail Gorbachev became leader of the USSR in March 1985, he inherited a system on the brink of collapse. Food was not reaching the shops and industry was unprofitable and out-of-date. He launched a series of reforms he called *perestroika* ("restructuring"). He wanted to modernize the entire complex of state farms and factories. To do this he needed the support of the whole nation. So for the first time, the Soviet Communist Party began to involve Soviet citizens in national policy. This new attitude was called *glasnost* ("openness"). Gorbachev also began to open up government. In 1989, elections were held all over the USSR to elect a council made up of deputies (representatives) from each republic. In many places, leading communists were defeated by radical reformers, such as Boris Yeltsin who became the deputy for Moscow. Nationalist candidates in republics that wanted independence from the USSR also achieved startling victories. The unity of the Soviet Union itself was coming under attack.

Statues of Lenin were pulled down all over Eastern Europe as communism collapsed.

THE COLD WAR THAWS

Nuclear weapons are very expensive to produce and, with the Soviet economy crumbling, Gorbachev could no longer compete in the arms race. In 1988, the Soviet Union and the USA agreed to reduce the production of nuclear weapons in an agreement called the INF Treaty.

Gorbachev and Ronald Reagan (President of the USA) shake hands on signing a treaty to reduce nuclear weapons.

EASTERN EUROPE REVOLTS

In Poland, in the summer of 1988, an illegal trade union called Solidarity organized a series of strikes throughout the country.

The Solidarity logo

Lech Walesa, the leader of Solidarity since 1980

In the days before Gorbachev came to power, the Soviet Union would have stepped in to crush any strikes or rebellions in the Soviet bloc. But Gorbachev had made it clear that he would not come to the aid of the Polish communist government. Without Soviet support, the Polish government was forced into talks with Solidarity and had to agree to the first free elections for forty years. In the summer of 1989, the Solidarity candidate, Tadeusz Mazowiecki, became the first non-communist prime minister in the Soviet bloc. In Hungary and Bulgaria, reforms took place from within the governing communist parties. Old style leaders were replaced with more liberal politicians. By 1990, free democratic elections had taken place in both countries.

The western side of the wall was covered with graffiti.

UNIFICATION OF GERMANY

Erich Honecker, head of the East German Communist Party since 1971, had always been a strict follower of Soviet policy. But he was not willing to follow the lead from Moscow and introduce reforms that might threaten his position.

The East German people, however, wanted change. Many thousands took advantage of the relaxed regime in nearby Hungary to emigrate to the West. At home, others began to protest against the government. Mass demonstrations were held and pro-democracy groups sprang up. On October 18, 1989, Honecker was forced to resign. His successor, Egon Krenz, hoped to lead a reforming, but still communist, government. He introduced wide-ranging reforms. Most dramatically, on November 9, 1989, he gave orders for the Berlin Wall to be pulled down. But this was not enough. In March 1990, full-scale elections were held and the democratic Christian Democrat Party gained power. They called for the rapid reunification of East and West Germany, in partnership with the Christian Democrat government in the West. At midnight on October 23, 1990, Germany was officially reunited.

East and West Berliners, united after nearly 30 years, celebrate on the Berlin Wall, November 1989.

CZECHOSLOVAKIA

In October 1968, Soviet troops had marched into Czechoslovakia to prevent a liberal government from introducing reforms. Since then the Czech regime had been closer to Stalinism than any other in Europe. But in the late 1980s, encouraged by events in the rest of Eastern Europe, Czech opposition to communism grew more open. A massive demonstration held in Prague in November 1989, set off a wave of protests across the country.

Vaclav Havel, founder of the main Czech anti-communist opposition group

Prague workers on strike, November 27, 1989

On November 27, the Czech government was forced to resign and elections were held the following June.

ROMANIA

Led by Nicolae Ceausescu since 1965, Romania had always been a special case among Soviet bloc countries. Ceausescu refused to follow the Soviet line on foreign policy and enforced his own particularly brutal form of communism.

Although events in the rest of Eastern Europe were ignored by the official Romanian media, in December 1989, a demonstration took place in the town of Timisoara. The state security force, *Securitate*, fired on the crowd.

A Romanian demonstrator waves the Romanian flag with the communist symbol cut out of it.

Exaggerated stories of hundreds of deaths spread to the capital, Bucharest. On December 21, a mass protest took place in front of the party headquarters. The Securitate opened fire on the crowd, but at this point the army chose to join the protesters. Bucharest became a battleground. Buildings were destroyed by gunfire and the streets were littered with hundreds of corpses. The Securitate were outnumbered and could not defend the government. On December 23, Ceausescu and his wife were captured. They were put on trial, found guilty and quickly executed.

Free elections were held in May 1990, and the National Salvation Front, a party of communists and ex-communists, came to power.

Later that year, there were unsuccessful attempts to replace the government with a more radical, entirely non-communist one.

THE BALTIC STATES

Nationalist groups within the USSR, particularly in the Baltic states of Latvia, Lithuania and Estonia, were encouraged by Gorbachev's unwillingness to intervene in the revolutions in Eastern Europe. In March 1990, Lithuania boldly declared itself independent. But Gorbachev was not prepared to see the USSR disintegrate. He set up an economic blockade, which stopped supplies of vital products, such as oil, from reaching the Baltic states. In January 1991, Soviet forces entered Latvia and Lithuania and tried to take control of their parliaments. Their attempt failed, however, and their actions only strengthened the determination of the nationalists.

THE END OF THE USSR

Politicians in the USSR were divided between hardliners, who wanted a communist Soviet Union to survive unchanged, and reformers, who believed in democratic reform and independence for the republics. Gorbachev was criticized by both sides. He wanted to hold the Union together but, as the republics began to take more independent action, he was forced to draw up the New Union Treaty. The treaty effectively signed away Moscow's control of the republics. This was too much for the hardliners. On August 19, 1990, the day before it was to be signed, they took control of the army and attempted to seize power.

Tanks were mobilized on the streets of Moscow. While Gorbachev was held prisoner in his summer house on the Black Sea, Boris Yeltsin led the resistance. He urged the people to go out on to the streets to defend democracy. Many responded and the army was reluctant to use force against them. On August 21, the leaders of the coup gave themselves up. Gorbachev was restored to power, but it was soon

Soviet tanks retreat from the streets of Moscow, August 21

clear that the reformers had won. At midnight on December 31, 1991, the Union of Soviet Socialist Republics officially ceased to exist. Gorbachev was out of a job and the red flag was removed from the Kremlin. Some Soviet republics immediately became independent, while others formed the Russian Federation, an alliance of semi-autonomous states, under the leadership of Boris Yeltsin.

EDUCATION

The idea of education for everyone is relatively new. Until the 19th century, most European children did not receive any sort of formal schooling. Children were taught only what they needed in order to survive in the community. Most boys had to provide for a family, so were taught how to farm or were apprenticed to a trade. Girls were taught domestic skills by their mothers, so that they could run their own homes or be employed as maids in the homes of other people.

THE FIRST SCHOOLS

All Greek pupils learned the Greek alphabet. This is the letter *pi*.

The Ancient Greeks were the first to establish schools in Europe, but only for boys. Greek education aimed to produce good citizens who could help with the government and protection of their city state, and add to its cultural life. But education was an expensive privilege many poorer citizens could not afford.

There were three different types of schools, for different subjects, and boys were expected to attend all of them.

A Greek poetry lesson

A rich family often employed a slave called a "paidagogos" to look after their son at school.

"Kitharistes" (music and poetry teacher)

One school taught writing and arithmetic. Another taught music and poetry. Boys were expected to learn long extracts of poetry by heart and to quote the great poets in conversation. In the third school, they were taught dancing and athletics, and they often took part in competitive games. For those with the ability and the money, there was also higher education.

This tradition of schooling was carried on by the Romans, and it spread throughout their empire. Teachers in Roman schools were often Greeks who had been captured and enslaved by the Roman army.

THE CHURCH TAKES OVER

An ornate letter "L" from a monastic manuscript

With the break-up of the Roman empire, the classical educational system collapsed. Learning survived only in the Church. Greek and Roman texts were preserved by monks in monasteries, and schools teaching Latin and Christian theology (the study of religion) were set up to train monks and priests. As these were the only schools, clergymen became the most educated people in Europe. Many found their way into the service of kings and princes, as tutors and powerful advisors.

By the 11th century, schools were beginning to admit boys (usually nobles' sons) who did not want to be priests, but simply wanted education. Nuns ran similar schools for girls. Village schools, run by parish priests, also sprang up. Here, poorer boys learned to read and write.

The Church also founded the first universities. Like the early schools, they were originally open only to the clergy. The earliest were Bologna (1088), Paris and Oxford (c.1150) and Cambridge (1209).

This painting from a 12th century manuscript shows a monk teaching at the University of Paris.

A NEW SPIRIT OF LEARNING

During the Renaissance (see page 22), education became much broader. The training of priests was still considered vital, but many people now believed it was also important for ordinary men to receive a good general education. A well-educated man would study such subjects as modern languages, literature, the sciences, music, singing and painting. Although women did not have the same opportunities, during the Renaissance it became easier for them to gain a limited formal education.

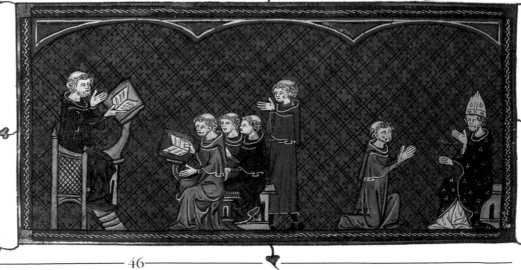

The hinged unit is folded, so the paper lies directly on the inked type block. It is then slid into position under the press's screw mechanism.

Paper

Apprentice

Inking pads

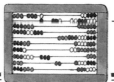

Universities were opened up and no longer taught only priests. Although only the rich could afford this extensive education, the invention of the printing press in the 15th century meant that books (once written by hand and very expensive) came within the reach of many more people. Learning and ideas began to spread more rapidly and easily throughout Europe.

A 15th century printing press

Screw

Type block

The type block is made up of a series of individual raised letters on small metal blocks.

Four type specimens

REFORMATION

In the 16th century, the Reformation (see page 19) broke the Roman Catholic Church's control over education in northern Europe. In many places it also made education available to more people. This was because Protestant clergy stressed the importance of learning for the individual. It taught that people could find out about God for themselves by reading the Bible, rather than relying on the Church's teachings. This meant that in Protestant countries even the poor were encouraged to read.

Protestant rulers naturally wanted all their subjects to share their new religion; to belong to a different faith could make someone a potential traitor. So these rulers insisted that their religion was taught in schools, using education as a way to convert people. Money for new schools was often provided by the sale of Catholic monasteries that had been forced to close.

In the early days of the Reformation, dissenters (people who belonged to a church other than that of the ruler) were forbidden to worship and were often persecuted. In many places they were also barred from education and so had to have their own special schools. In some places, this survived until well into the 19th century.

SCHOOLS FOR ALL

The Enlightenment (see page 25) and the French Revolution (see page 26) further weakened the Church's grip on education, shaping the idea of education for the poor as well as the rich. Many charities were established at this time, which set up schools to educate poorer children. In the 19th century, groups of liberal thinkers campaigned for education to be provided by governments. But many European monarchs were suspicious of educational reformers, because they also questioned such things as the power of kings and the privileges of the nobility.

A 19th century charity school. In most schools boys and girls were taught separately. .

With the spread of industrialization, however, governments were forced to take education more seriously. People needed a basic education in order to carry out increasingly technical factory work. Many countries, including Austria, Russia, Spain and the newly united Germany, were forced to introduce state education. It was needed to keep up with modern science, industry and technology, which were essential for the nation's economy. Many parents, however, were against their children going to school, as it meant they could no longer bring in a much needed income. But pressure from reformers and economic necessity meant that education gradually became available to all. By the middle of the 20th century, all governments in Europe had set up some form of compulsory state education for both boys and girls.

In England, inspectors were employed to catch children not at school.

EDUCATION AS PROPAGANDA

Before the 20th century, education tended to be controlled by the churches (both Roman Catholic and Protestant). State education shifted this control to government and provided political parties with the opportunity to use schools for their own benefit. In communist and fascist countries in particular, governments forced schools to teach all subjects in a way that justified the government's own political and economic policies. This 1972 Soviet poster bearing the slogan "Knowledge for all! Youth exposes imperialism" shows how the Soviet authorities used education as a political tool.

ARCHITECTURE

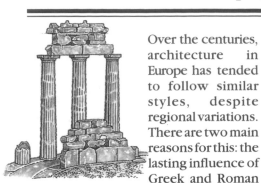

Ruins of a classical temple at Delphi, Greece

Over the centuries, architecture in Europe has tended to follow similar styles, despite regional variations. There are two main reasons for this: the lasting influence of Greek and Roman architecture and the dominance of Christianity. From the fall of the Roman empire until the Renaissance, most major building projects were for the Church, and it was through the Church that many architectural ideas were carried over the continent.

CLASSICAL ARCHITECTURE

Classical Greek architecture (see page 10), with its emphasis on symmetry and harmony, was adopted by the Romans who spread the style throughout their empire. The Romans also introduced new techniques and forms, such as the dome, the vault and the use of concrete, which allowed them to build bigger, more monumental, structures.

Much of their architecture was destroyed by the barbarian tribes who invaded the Roman empire. Building skills were lost, as Europe entered a period of turmoil. But despite this destruction, there were enough ruins surviving to inspire later generations. Classical architectural styles have been revived repeatedly throughout history.

EASTERN EUROPEAN ARCHITECTURE

After the fall of Rome, eastern Europe came under the influence of the Byzantine empire and the eastern Church. Eastern European architecture developed its own style, distinct from that in the west. Byzantine churches were built on a Greek-cross plan (a cross with four arms of equal length). There was usually a dome built over the area where the two arms met.

Floor plan of a Byzantine church

One of the most important innovations of Byzantine architects was a new method of supporting domes on four curved triangles, called pendentives, that met in a ring over four pillars and arches. This allowed bigger domes to be built, without using very heavy supports below to hold them up. One of the greatest examples of the pendentive dome is in the Church of St. Sophia (today a museum) in Constantinople (now Istanbul). A massive dome 31.2m (107ft) in diameter seems to float unsupported over the square space below (see below).

Byzantine churches also had their own style of interior decoration. Ceilings and walls were completely covered with lavish mosaics and painted murals.

The inside of the dome of St. Sophia (c.550)

Different parts of eastern Europe developed their own versions of the Byzantine style. One of the most distinctive variations was in Russia, where they used an onion-shaped dome which swelled in the middle before coming to a point. This form appears to have developed in northern Russia, where traditional domes collapsed under the weight of snow.

St. Basil's Cathedral (1550-60) in Moscow, a flamboyant example of an onion-domed church. It was built by Tsar Ivan the Terrible to celebrate his military victories.

ROMANESQUE

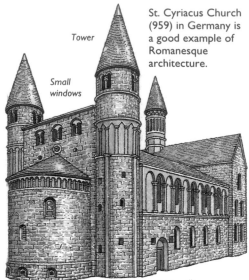

Tower

Small windows

St. Cyriacus Church (959) in Germany is a good example of Romanesque architecture.

Thick walls

In the 10th century, a new style of architecture, which we call Romanesque, developed in western Europe. It grew out of the early medieval obsession with defending property and keeping out intruders. Every building, whether castle or church, was built as a stronghold, with thick walls, small windows, short columns and semicircular arches. This reflects the centuries of conflict that Europe had suffered since the fall of Rome. But this new style of architecture was also a sign that a more stable society was being established. The barbarians who had sacked the cities of the Roman empire had settled down, set up kingdoms and accepted the authority of the Pope. It was a symbol of a new Europe: medieval Christendom.

"Onion" domes (painted in the 17th century)

The exterior of the cathedral was covered with bright tiling in the 17th century, giving it an Oriental appearance.

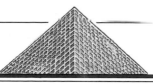

GOTHIC

Gothic window from Chartres, in France

In the 12th century, the Romanesque style began to be replaced by a new one, later known as Gothic. It was characterized by lighter, taller, more delicate-looking churches. Its aim was to use light and colour to make churches a symbol of heaven on Earth. The movement began in France, from where it spread throughout Europe. In Gothic churches columns were taller and narrower, more wall space was used for stained glass windows and the semicircular Romanesque arches were replaced with pointed arches.

RENAISSANCE TO BAROQUE

In the 14th century, the Renaissance led to a revival of classical architecture. Like the Greeks, Renaissance architects used mathematics to create harmony and proportion. The growth of towns and trade at this time meant that many non-Church buildings sprang up. Architects built grand villas for merchants and bankers wanting to display their importance in society (see page 22).

By the late Renaissance, some architects, particularly in Catholic countries, were finding classical forms restricting. A new style developed called Baroque. Baroque architects concentrated on the elaborate decoration of classical forms.

A Baroque column: essentially classical in structure but highly decorated with fine carvings

NEO-CLASSICISM AND 19TH CENTURY REVIVALS

In the 18th century, there was a reaction against the extravagance of the Baroque style. European architects again focused on the simplicity of classical buildings in a style known as neo-classicism. During the French Revolution (see page 26), neo-classicism came to have a political significance. While Baroque architecture was linked with corruption and the aristocracy, neo-classical buildings were seen as a symbol of equality and republicanism.

In the 19th century, other styles, such as Gothic, were also revived. Many buildings were pastiches, imitating styles from different periods.

ART NOUVEAU

Toward the end of the 19th century, a new form of architecture emerged, called *Art Nouveau*. It was not based on any past style, although it was influenced by Japanese painting. Symmetry was often abandoned, and sinuously flowing shapes and flame-like lines were used instead of straight edges and right angles. Although *Art Nouveau* only lasted for a relatively short period, it had a great influence on many different forms of design: interior decoration, magazines, advertising and the design of everyday household objects such as lamps.

An *Art Nouveau* lamp post in Paris

MODERNISM AND BEYOND

At the beginning of the 20th century, a new movement began in Austria, Germany and America which became known as modernism, or the International Style. Modernist architects emphasized the function of a building rather than concentrating on its decoration. They made use of technological advances in materials such as glass, steel and reinforced concrete. In 1919, Walter Gropius, a German modernist architect, founded a school of

design called the Bauhaus.

In 1922, the school moved to the city of Dessau, where Gropius designed the school's new buildings, according to modernist principles.

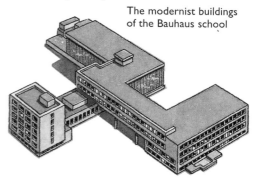

The modernist buildings of the Bauhaus school

The French architect Le Corbusier developed this style and adapted it for domestic architecture. He wanted to create low-cost, functional and comfortable housing for poor workers.

Since the Second World War, some architects have applied modernist ideas to highly original buildings, such as the Centre Pompidou in Paris. Designed by two architects, Richard Rogers and Renzo Piano, it displays on the outside of the building the parts that are usually hidden, such as the escalators, plumbing and air-conditioning. Others have reacted against the harshness of modernism and have borrowed from more traditional styles, such as classicism. These architects are known as post-modernists.

The Centre Pompidou in Paris is one of the most eccentric modernist buildings.

SCIENCE

18th century English microscope

Europe has a long tradition of scientific research and discovery which dates back to the Ancient Greeks. By the 1900s, European scientists had formulated many of the essential laws of physics, chemistry and biology.

The economic damage left by two world wars, however, has meant that Europe has played a less crucial role in scientific progress in the 20th century. Many modern developments have come from the USA or are the work of international teams, pooling information.

THE ANCIENT GREEKS

Many of the scientific theories developed by the Ancient Greeks became the basis for later research and discovery. The Greek philosophers (see page 10) believed that the world was an ordered system, with laws which could be understood by rational thought and study.

This Roman mosaic shows Greek students at the Academy, a school in Athens founded by the philosopher Plato.

One of the best known Greek philosophers is Aristotle (384-322BC). He stressed the importance of observation in scientific study. One of his theories was that the universe was arranged in a series of spheres around a spherical Earth. This was accepted by many for more than 1000 years. Hippocrates (c.450-370BC) is often known as the "father of medicine". He rejected the belief of many early people that illness was a punishment from the gods. Instead he studied symptoms to find the causes of diseases.

MEDIEVAL SCIENCE

The Romans adopted many Greek ideas. But, after the fall of their empire, many of these were forgotten and progress was slow. In western Europe, education was controlled by the Roman Catholic Church, which did not encourage scientific study. Those who challenged the Church's account of the world often risked persecution.

When the Muslims conquered Spain in the 8th century, they brought with them scientific works they had copied from the Greeks, as well as discoveries of their own. By the end of the 11th century, many of these works were known to European scholars. The Muslims had also adopted several Chinese inventions, including the magnetic compass and gunpowder, which they introduced into Europe.

The Muslims put many of their ideas to practical use. For example, they taught Europeans how to use wind and water to power mills and pumps. A large part of the Netherlands was created using windmills to pump water out of the vast marshes at the mouth of the Rhine.

A 16th century Dutch windmill used for draining land

Sails arranged in a cross

Thatched base

THE GROWTH OF SCIENCE

Renaissance scholars challenged many established views of the world. In 1543, a Polish astronomer called Copernicus broke with classical thinking with his revolutionary theory that the Sun, rather than the Earth, was at the heart of the universe. Later astronomers, such as the German, Johannes Kepler, and the Italian, Galileo Galilei, studied Copernicus's ideas and took them further.

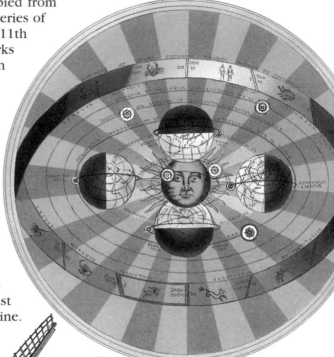

Kepler's view of the solar system. His study showed that the planets moved around the Sun in extended circular paths called ellipses.

Andreas Vesalius, a pharmacist from Brussels who studied at Padua University, was the first scholar to make a detailed study of the human body. In 1543, he published *The Fabric of the Human Body*, which contained detailed drawings of human bones and muscles. His book transformed anatomy (the study of the human body) into a well-respected academic pursuit.

A drawing from Vesalius's book

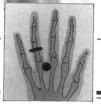

A statue of Newton (1642-1727)

In the 16th and 17th centuries, the use of experiments became more important as a scientific method. Until then, many scientific ideas had been based on religion or philosophy. Science flourished, especially in England, where Isaac Newton discovered the laws of gravity, Robert Hooke discovered the biological cell and Robert Boyle made important discoveries about the properties of gases.

With the growth of experiments, chemistry (the study of the substances that make up the world) developed into a modern science. During the 18th century, many discoveries were made about how substances react under different conditions. In 1808, John Dalton proved the theory that all substances were made up of tiny particles, which we call atoms. This became the basis for modern chemistry.

Apparatus used by Dalton

In the 1820s, Michael Faraday discovered that magnets could be used to create electric currents. This led to the invention of the electric motor and the development of electricity for use in industry and the home.

X-RAYS AND THE ATOMIC AGE

In Germany in 1895, Wilhelm Röntgen observed that, under special conditions, electric currents gave out rays which made certain chemicals glow. He named them "x-rays". Röntgen found that, if directed through a body, x-rays created a photographic image of the bones.

In 1896, a French physicist, Antoine Becquerel, discovered that the atoms of certain substances, which we call radioactive, gave out powerful rays and were themselves a source of energy. This greatly contributed to the understanding of the atom. In 1905, Albert Einstein produced some radical theories which re-examined some of the most fundamental ideas about science. His work on atoms and atomic particles led to the development of the atomic bomb (see page 37).

FIGHTING DISEASE

Until the 18th century, little was understood about what caused disease and how to cure it. But, in 1796, an English doctor called Edward Jenner showed the value of vaccination, the process by which someone is protected from an illness by being injected with a milder version of the disease.

In the 1850s, a French chemist, Louis Pasteur, discovered that some diseases were caused by tiny organisms called bacteria. This led to the use of antiseptics (substances which kill bacteria outside the body) by an English surgeon, Joseph Lister. This was one of the most major advances in medicine in the 19th century. It meant that surgical equipment could be sterilized for operations, so reducing the risk of the patient's wounds becoming infected.

This work was continued by Alexander Fleming, a Scottish doctor. In 1928, he discovered penicillin, a substance that can kill germs inside the body. Penicillin

This illustration shows Lister directing an antiseptic operation.

was produced in large quantities for the first time in the 1940s. It was the first of a group of drugs known as antibiotics. Antibiotics have had an enormous effect on modern medicine. Diseases that used to be potentially fatal, such as typhoid, can now be cured quite easily.

Penicillin through a microscope

EVOLUTION

This cartoon mocks Darwin's theory that people may have evolved from apes.

In 1859, Charles Darwin, an English naturalist, published *On the Origin of Species by Means of Natural Selection.* This book set out his theory that all living things had evolved over millions of years. It caused an uproar, because it challenged the biblical story that the world had remained unchanged since its creation. Today most scientists believe in some form of evolution, although there is still much evidence to be found.

THE SCIENCE OF LIFE

In the mid 19th century, an Austrian priest called Gregor Mendel carried out a series of experiments with pea plants. He showed that certain characteristics were passed on from one generation of plant to the next. Mendel suggested that these were controlled by units, which we now call genes. This was the beginning of a new science, called genetics. One of the most important breakthroughs in genetics was made in England in 1953. Francis Crick and James Watson built a scale model of a molecule, called DNA, which carries genes within the cells of every living thing.

EUROPE IN THE 1990S

This map shows Europe in 1993. It reflects the upheavals that have beset the continent throughout the 20th century. In 1914, the map of Europe looked like a simple jigsaw made up of a few large empires and nation states. But two world wars and the collapse of the Soviet bloc left it fragmented into many smaller units. By 1993, the map of Europe was an irregular mosaic of small states.

Western Europe has remained relatively unchanged since 1914. But the national boundaries within eastern and central Europe have been redrawn several times. Since the First World War, seventeen nation states have been created in the area.

The main force behind the reshaping of Europe has come from demands for independence from minortity groups. For example, in the early 1990s, Slovenia, Croatia, Bosnia and Hercegovina, and Macedonia all broke away from Yugoslavia. In the independent state of Bosnia and Hercegovina, a civil war broke out as different factions disputed their rights to territory. In 1992, Czechoslovakia divided into the two states of the Czech Republic and Slovakia.

Some people think that in the future Europe will break down into even smaller units. In western Europe, the national parliaments of countries such as France, Italy and Belgium are giving more and more powers to local governments. This may eventually lead to independent regions, possible under the authority of the European Community. In eastern Europe, there are continuing demands for independence from other minority groups. The Montenegrins, for example, are trying to gain independence from the Serbians, who control what remains of Yugoslavia.

FINLAND

RUSSIA

SWEDEN

●Helsinki

○St. Petersburg

●Tallinn

●Stockholm

ESTONIA

LATVIA

●Riga

●Moscow

LITHUANIA

●Vilnius

RUS.

●Minsk

BELARUS

POLAND

●Warsaw

UKRAINE

●Kiev

Prague

REPUBLIC

SLOVAKIA

enna ●Bratislava

MOLDOVA

●Kishinëv

IA ●Budapest

HUNGARY

●Zagreb

ana

ROMANIA

●Belgrade

●Bucharest

BOSNIA AND
HERCEGOVINA

●Sarajevo

BULGARIA

YUGOSLAVIA

●Sofia

●Skopje

MACEDONIA

●Tirane

ALBANIA

●Istanbul

TURKEY

GREECE

●Athens

Rhodes ·

CYPRUS

●Nicosia

les

ALTA

lletta

Crete

● Capital city

○ Other major city

DID YOU KNOW?

Russia is the biggest country in the world, covering 17,075,500km² (6,591,000 square miles), but only a fraction of this area is in Europe. The biggest country with all its borders in Europe is the Ukraine at 604,000km² (233,000 square miles).

The smallest country in the world is the Vatican City, which is situated in the middle of the Italian capital, Rome. At under half a square kilometre (under one third of a square mile), it is too small to be shown on this map. It is the property of the Roman Catholic Church.

Iceland is the most sparsely populated country in Europe, with 260,000 people living in 103,000km² (40,000 square miles).

Monaco, a tiny independent state in the south of France, is the most crowded country in Europe, with 30,000 people inhabiting only 2km² (0.8 square miles).

Bonn lost its status as a capital city when East and West Germany were united in 1990. Berlin, formerly the capital of East Germany, became the capital of united Germany.

Most of Turkey is in Asia, but its north-western corner (shown on the map in pink), which lies to the west of a stretch of water called the Bosphorus, is in Europe.

The Bosphorus dissects the Turkish city of Istanbul, which lies half in Europe and half in Asia.

Although the capital of the Netherlands is Amsterdam, the Dutch parliament meets in the city of The Hague.

53

EUROPEAN DATA

	Local name	Capital city	Main languages spoken	Population
Albania	Shqîpëri	Tiranë	Albanian	3,262,000
Andorra	Andorra	Andorra la Vella	Catalan, French	51,000
Austria	Österreich	Vienna	German	7,623,000
Belarus	Belarus	Minsk	Belorussian	10,200,000
Belgium	Belgique(French), België (Flemish),	Brussels	Flemish, French	9,958,000
Bosnia and Hercegovina	Bosna Hercegovina	Sarajevo	Serbo-Croat	4,364,500
Bulgaria	Bãlgarija	Sofia	Bulgarian	8,997,000
Croatia	Hrvatska	Zagreb	Serbo-Croat	4,763,000
Cyprus	Kipros (Greek), Kibris (Turkish)	Nicosia	Greek, Turkish	568,000
Czech Republic	Ceská Republika	Prague	Czech, Slovak	10,320,000
Denmark	Danmark	Copenhagen	Danish	5,139,000
Estonia	Eesti	Tallinn	Estonian, Russian	1,600,000
Finland	Suomi	Helsinki	Finnish, Swedish	4,978,000
France	France	Paris	French	56,647,000
Germany	Bundesrepublik Deutschland	Berlin	German	79,113,000
Greece	Ellás	Athens	Greek	10,038,000
Hungary	Magyarország	Budapest	Hungarian	10,340,000
Iceland	Ísland	Reykjavík	Icelandic	254,000
Ireland	Eire	Dublin	Irish, English	3,509,000
Italy	Italia	Rome	Italian	57,512,000
Latvia	Latvija	Riga	Latvian, Russian	2,700,000
Liechtenstein	Liechtenstein	Vaduz	German	28,700
Lithuania	Lietuva	Vilnius	Lithuanian, Russian	3,700,000
Luxembourg	Lëtzebuerg (Letz.) Luxembourg (Fr.) Luxemburg (Ger.)	Luxembourg	French, German, Letzebuergesch	379,000
Macedonia	Macedonia	Skopje	Macedonian	2,111,000
Malta	Malta	Valletta	English, Maltese	353,000
Moldova	Moldova	Kishinëv	Romanian	4,400,000
Monaco	Monaco	Monaco	French	29,300
Netherlands	Nederland	Amsterdam	Dutch	14,934,000
Norway	Norge	Oslo	Norwegian	4,246,000
Poland	Polska	Warsaw	Polish	38,070,000
Portugal	Portugal	Lisbon	Portuguese	10,388,000
Romania	Romãnia	Bucharest	Romanian	23,265,000
Russia	Rossiya	Moscow	Russian	147,400,000
Slovakia	Slovenska	Bratislava	Slovak, Czech, Magyar	5,264,000
Slovenia	Slovenija	Ljubljana	Slovenian	1,950,000
Spain	España	Madrid	Spanish, Catalan, Basque, Galician	39,618,000
Sweden	Sverige	Stockholm	Swedish	8,529,000
Switzerland	Schweiz (Ger.) Suisse (Fr.) Svizzera (It.)	Berne	French, German, Italian, Romansch	6,756,000
Ukraine	Ukraine	Kiev	Ukrainian	51,700,000
United Kingdom	United Kingdom	London	English	57,384,000
Vatican City	Città del Vaticano	Vatican City	Italian, Latin	750
Yugoslavia	Jugoslavija	Belgrade	Serbo-Croat	9,831,000

Currency	Main religions	Main ethnic groups living there	Area Sq. km	Sq. miles
1 Lek = 100 qintars	Muslim	Albanians, Greeks	29,000	11,000
French Franc, Spanish Peseta	Roman Catholic	Catalans, Spanish, French	500	193
1 Schilling = 100 groschen	Roman Catholic	Germans, Slovenes, Croatians	84,000	32,500
Belarussian Rouble	Roman Catholic, Russian Orthodox	Belarussians, Russians	207,000	80,000
1 Belgian Franc = 100 centimes	Roman Catholic	Flemings, Walloons (French speakers)	31,000	12,000
1 Yugoslav Dinar = 100 paras	Eastern Orthodox, Roman Catholic, Muslim	Serbs (Christian and Muslim), Croatians (Christian and Muslim)	51,000	20,000
1 Lev = 100 stotinki	Eastern Orthodox, Muslim	Bulgarians, Turks	111,000	43,000
1 Croatian Dinar = 100 paras	Roman Catholic, Eastern Orthodox	Croatians, Serbs	56,000	22,000
1 Cyprus Pound = 100 cents	Eastern Orthodox, Muslim	Greeks, Turks	9,000	3,500
1 Koruna = 100 haler	Roman Catholic	Czechs, Slovaks	79,000	305,000
1 Danish Krone = 100 øre	Protestant	Danes	43,000	16,500
Kroon	Protestant	Estonians, Russians	45,000	17,500
1 Markka = 100 penni	Protestant	Finns, Swedes, Lapps	337,000	130,000
1 French Franc = 100 centimes	Roman Catholic	French, North Africans	551,000	212,500
1 Deutsche Mark = 100 Pfennige	Roman Catholic, Protestant	Germans, Turks	357,000	138,000
1 Drachma = 100 leptae	Eastern Orthodox	Greeks	132,000	51,000
1 Forint = 100 fillér	Roman Catholic	Hungarians, Germans, Gypsies	93,000	36,000
1 Króna = 100 aurar	Protestant	Icelanders	103,000	40,000
1 Irish Pound = 100 new pence	Roman Catholic	Irish, English	70,000	27,000
Italian Lira	Roman Catholic	Italians, Germans, Slovenes, Albanians	301,000	116,000
Lat	Protestant	Latvians, Russians	25,000	9,500
1 Swiss Franc = 100 centimes	Roman Catholic	Alemannics (Germanic people), Italians	160	62
Litas	Roman Catholic	Lithuanians, Russians, Poles	65,000	25,000
1 Luxembourg Franc = 100 centimes	Roman Catholic	Luxembourgers	3,000	1,000
1 Yugoslav Dinar = 100 paras	Eastern Orthodox	Macedonians	25,700	9,920
1 Maltese Lira = 100 cents	Roman Catholic	Italians, Arabs, French	300	116
Lei	Russian Orthodox	Moldavians, Ukranians, Russians, Jews	33,700	13,000
1 French Franc = 100 centimes	Roman Catholic	French, Italians, Monegasques	2	0.8
1 Dutch Guilder = 100 cents	Roman Catholic, Protestant	Dutch	37,000	14,500
1 Norwegian Krone = 100 øre	Protestant	Norwegians, Lapps	324,000	125,000
1 Zloty = 100 groszy	Roman Catholic	Poles, Germans, Ukranians, Belarussians	313,000	121,000
Escudo	Roman Catholic	Portuguese, North Africans	92,000	35,000
1 Leu = 100 bani	Eastern Orthodox	Romanians, Hungarians, Germans	238,000	92,000
1 Rouble = 100 kopecks	Russian Orthodox	Russians	17,075,500	6,591,000
1 Koruna = 100 haler	Roman Catholic	Slovaks, Czechs	49,000	19,000
Tolar	Roman Catholic	Slovenes	20,500	8,000
Peseta	Roman Catholic	Spanish, Catalans, Galicians, Basques	505,000	195,000
1 Swedish Krona = 100 øre	Protestant	Swedes, Finns, Lapps	450,000	174,000
1 Swiss Franc = 100 centimes Romansch	Roman Catholic, Protestant	Swiss, other central Europeans	41,000	16,000
Karbovanet	Roman Catholic	Ukrainians, Russians	604,000	233,000
1 Pound Sterling = 100 new pence	Protestant	English, Irish, Scottish, Welsh, West Indians, Asians	244,000	94,000
Italian Lira	Roman Catholic	Italians, Swiss	0.4	0.1
1 Yugoslav Dinar = 100 paras	Eastern Orthodox	Serbs	102,170	39,450

DATE CHART

c.30,000BC *Homo sapiens* first appears in Europe.

c.18,000BC Cave walls at Lascaux, France, decorated with hunting scenes.

c.6000BC Groups of farmers from Asia Minor settle on the island of Crete and the Greek mainland.

c.5200-2000BC Farming spreads through western and northern Europe.

c.2000-1450BC Minoan civilization in Crete.

c.1600-1050BC Mycenaean civilization in Greece.

753BC Traditional date for the founding of Rome.

510-09BC Rome becomes a republic.

508BC Democracy introduced in Athens.

c.500BC Celts begin migrating from central Europe to Spain, Britain, Ireland and the Low Countries.

c.500-338BC Classical period in Greek art.

336-323BC Alexander the Great rules a vast empire.

146BC Roman territory expands to include Carthaginian lands in north Africa and southern Europe. Start of Roman rule in Greece.

27BC End of Roman Republic.

c.4BC Birth of Jesus of Nazareth.

98-117 Roman empire reaches its greatest extent under Emperor Trajan.

c.200 Germanic tribes begin invading Roman empire.

c.370 Huns invade Europe, pushing Germanic tribes deeper into Roman territory.

395 Roman empire becomes permanently split between east and west.

c.400-500 Germanic tribes overrun western Europe and establish kingdoms.

413 Power in Rome is taken over by the Pope (the bishop of Rome).

455 Vandals (a Germanic tribe) sack Rome.

476 Western Roman empire comes to an end.

c.500-700 Slavs migrate from central Europe to Russia.

527-65 Reign of Emperor Justinian of the Eastern Roman (or Byzantine) empire.

c.570 Birth of Mohammed in Mecca in the Middle East.

596 St. Augustine is sent to Britain by the Pope to convert the Saxons to Christianity.

c.680 Bulgars invade the Balkans, intermarry with the Slavs and establish a Bulgar state.

711 Muslim Arabs conquer much of Spain.

732 Battle of Poitiers: advancing Arabs are defeated in southwest France.

768-814 Rule of Charlemagne.

793 Vikings from Scandinavia begin raiding Europe.

815 Slav kingdom of Croatia established.

830 Slav kingdom of Moravia established.

832-47 Vikings settle in Ireland.

862 St. Cyril and St. Methodius of the Orthodox Church convert Slavs to Christianity.

c.862 Principality of Russia established by the Swedish warrior, Rurik.

870 Charlemagne's empire is divided into a western kingdom (France) and an eastern kingdom (Germany).

c.890-930 Norway is first organized as a single kingdom.

960 Slav tribes of northern Poland unite to form a Polish state.

962 Otto I of Germany crowned Holy Roman Emperor and becomes founder of Holy Roman Empire.

990-92 Poland switches its allegiance from the Orthodox Church to the Catholic Church.

From1000 Scandinavians converted to Christianity.

c.1000 Leif Ericsson reaches America.

1014-35 Canute, king of Denmark, rules an empire which covers Denmark, England, Norway and part of Sweden.

1035 Poland falls under the authority of the Holy Roman Empire.
Norwegian kingdom is restored.

c.1050 Romanesque architecture flourishes in Europe.

1054 Schism (split) between the Roman Catholic Church and the Eastern Orthodox Church, caused by the Pope's claim to supremacy over the whole Christian Church.

1066 William of Normandy conquers England and becomes King William I.

1071 Turks capture Jerusalem from Byzantines.

1086 Bohemia is recognized as a kingdom by the Holy Roman Emperor.

1094 Portugal becomes independent.

1096-99 First Crusade.

1100-1400 City republics in Italy and Germany grow in power.

1137-44 St. Denis, the first Gothic cathedral, is built in Paris.

1147-49 Second Crusade.

c.1150 Paris University founded.

1168 Oxford University founded.

1189-92 Third Crusade.

1191-94 Sicily becomes part of the Holy Roman Empire.

1204 Fourth Crusade.

1212 Kings of Castile, Aragon and Navarre defeat Arabs in Spain.

1215 *Magna Carta* signed in England.

1237-40 Mongols invade Russia.

1241 Mongols invade Hungary and Poland.

1249 Swedish rule extended to Finland.

1309-78 The papacy moves to Avignon and falls under the influence of the French kings.

1337-1453 The Hundred Years War between France and England. They quarrel over territory and the right to the French crown.

1347-1351 The Black Death kills over one third of the population of Europe.

1354 Ottoman Turks acquire Gallipoli, their first European territory.

1387	Geoffrey Chaucer, the first great poet in modern English, writes *The Canterbury Tales.*	**1611**	English trading company establishes trading post in India.
1389	Ottoman Turks gain control of the Balkans.	**1614-36**	Europeans begin to discover Australia.
1397	Scandinavia is united under one ruler, Margaret, queen of Denmark and Norway.	**1616**	Dutch and French set up trading posts in West Africa.
1436	The Italian architect, Leon Baptista Alberti, describes the laws of perspective for drawing.	**1618-48**	Thirty Years War fought between Protestant provinces and Catholic imperial forces in the Holy Roman Empire. German Protestants curb the power of the ruling Catholics.
1452	Birth of Leonardo da Vinci.		
1453	Ottoman Turks capture Constantinople and the Byzantine empire comes to an end.		
1455	Johann Gutenberg publishes the *Gutenberg Bible,* the first printed book in Europe.	**1620**	English Puritans sail from Plymouth to North America on the *Mayflower.*
1456-67	Ottomans take over the Balkan states.	**1626**	Dutch found New Amsterdam (now New York).
1469	Ferdinand of Aragon marries Isabella of Castile Their kingdoms are united in 1479.	**1628**	William Harvey publishes his discovery of the circulation of the blood.
1480	Ivan III declares himself first Tsar of Russia.	**1637**	English establish a trading post in China.
1485	Alberti's theories on Renaissance architecture are published	**1642-48**	English Civil War.
		1643-45	War between Denmark and Sweden. Sweden becomes the major power in the Baltic.
1488	Bartholmeu Diaz sails to the Cape of Good Hope.		
1492	Christopher Columbus reaches the West Indies. Ferdinand and Isabella conquer the last Arab kingdom in Spain.	**1643-1715**	Reign of Louis XIV.
		1646	Swedes take Prague and invade Bavaria.
		1648	Spain recognizes the United Provinces.
1494	The Pope divides New World (South America) into Portuguese and Spanish empires.	**1649**	Charles I executed. Britain becomes a republic.
		1654-57	War between Russia and Poland. Russia takes Polish territory.
1497	John Cabot sails from England to Newfoundland.		
1498	Vasco da Gama makes first European sea voyage to India.	**1660**	British monarchy restored under Charles II.
		1661	Robert Boyle defines chemical elements.
1499	Switzerland establishes independence from the Holy Roman Empire.	**1664**	Turks invade and occupy Hungary.
		1665	Isaac Newton discovers gravity.
1510	Ferdinand of Aragon and Castile takes the kingdom of Navarre. Spain is united.	**1668**	Isaac Newton invents the reflecting telescope.
		1676	Turks win Polish Ukraine.
1517	Martin Luther begins the Reformation.	**1679**	Russia wins Ukraine from Turkey.
1519	Charles V of Spain becomes Holy Roman Emperor.	**1683**	Ottoman Turks fail to take Vienna. Turkish power in Europe starts to decline.
1519-22	Magellan and Elcano sail from Spain around the world.		
		1687	Turks lose Hungary. Hungary becomes a possession of the Hapsburg family, the emperors of Austria.
1531	Copernicus puts forward his theory that the Sun, not the Earth, is at the heart of the universe.		
1541	Hungary becomes a province of Turkey.	**1689-1725**	Reign of Tsar Peter the Great of Russia. Russia becomes a major European power.
1545	Catholic Church meets at Trento to discuss its reaction to the Reformation.		
		1694	Birth of Voltaire, the French enlightenment philosopher.
1555	Philip of Spain inherits the Netherlands (part of the Holy Roman Empire).		
		1699	Austrians recover Ottoman-held territory in the Balkans. Poles win back the Ukraine.
1557-82	Russia, Poland, Sweden and Denmark fight over Baltic territories.		
1581	Russia begins the conquest of Siberia.	**1701**	Elector of Brandenburg becomes king of Prussia.
	The northern provinces of the Netherlands declare themselves independent from Spain as the United Provinces.	**1703**	Peter the Great founds city of St. Petersburg.
		1707	Union of Scotland and England, renamed Great Britain.
c.1590	William Shakespeare starts writing his first plays.	**1756-63**	Seven Years War caused by rivalry between Austria and Prussia in Europe and between France and Britain in the colonies.
1596	Galileo Galilei invents the thermometer. Dutch establish trading bases in Far East.		
1603	French start to colonize North America.	**1762**	Mozart, aged six, makes his first professional tour of Europe as a pianist.
1607	First permanent English settlement in North America.		
		1763	Peace of Paris ends the Seven Years War, leaving Britain as a major colonial power and Austria as the strongest power in central Europe.
1608	Hans Lippershey invents the telescope.		
1609	Johannes Kepler explains how planets orbit the Sun.	**1767**	The *Spinning Jenny* is invented by James Hargreaves.

1769	Richard Arkwright invents the water-frame, a water powered spinning machine.
1770	Birth of the German composer, Beethoven, in Bonn.
1771	Russia conquers the Crimea and destroys the Turkish fleet.
1772	First Partition of Poland by Russia, Prussia and Austria.
1776	Thirteen colonies of North America sign the Declaration of Independence.
1782	James Watt invents an efficient steam engine.
1783	Britain recognizes American independence.
1784	British government takes control of political affairs in British India.
1788	Convicts transported from Britain to Sydney, the first permanent British settlement in Australia.
1789	Storming of the Bastille and start of the French Revolution.
1792	France becomes a republic and declares war on Austria and Prussia.
1793	Execution of Louis XVI of France and his wife Marie-Antoinette.
	France declares war on Britain, the Netherlands and Spain.
	Second Partition of Poland. Russia and Prussia take more Polish territory.
1795	Coalition of European powers formed against France.
	Third Partition of Poland. What is left of Poland is divided up between Austria, Prussia and Russia.
1796	Edward Jenner introduces vaccination against smallpox.
1804	Napoleon crowns himself Emperor of France.
1804-13	Serbs revolt against Ottoman rule.
1806	Napoleon dissolves the Holy Roman Empire.
1808-25	Wars of independence in South and Central America. Argentina, Paraguay, Venezuela, Colombia, Uruguay and Chile all win independence from Spain and Portugal.
1809	Russia wins Finland from Sweden.
1810	Napoleon controls much of western Europe.
1812	France invades Russia, but is forced to retreat.
1815	Napoleon defeated at Battle of Waterloo.
	The Congress of Vienna meets to settle post-war boundaries and other problems.
1825	First passenger steam train opens in England between Stockton and Darlington.
1829	Greeks win independence from Turkey, and Russia makes gains in the Balkans.
1830	Belgian uprising against Dutch leads to Belgian independence.
1832	Reform Act in Britain gives the vote to middle class men.
1848	Year of Revolutions. Liberal and nationalist revolutions break out in Sicily, Paris, Venice, Vienna, Berlin, Milan, Warsaw and Prague.
1848	Karl Marx's *Communist Manifesto* published.
1854-56	Crimean War. Russia demands a protectorate over Turkish Christians and use of Dardanelles for Russian warships. Russia is defeated by Turkey, Britain and France and forced to give up some territory.
1859	Charles Darwin outlines his theory of evolution.
1860	Italian states of Parma, Modena, Tuscany, the Papal States and Sicily unite with Piedmont to form an Italian kingdom. The Pope keeps Rome.
1862	Louis Pasteur shows that disease is caused by germs.
1866	War between Austria and Italy. Italy gains Venice. Mendel publishes his laws of inheritance.
1867	Austrian Empire is renamed Austro-Hungarian Empire, after Hungary is given equal status with Austria as the Dual Monarchy.
1869	The Russian novelist, Tolstoy, completes *War and Peace.*
1870	Rome falls to the Italian Kingdom and becomes its capital city. The Pope keeps the Vatican.
1871	William I of Prussia becomes emperor of a united Germany.
1874	Iceland wins independence from Denmark.
1877-78	Romania, Montenegro and Serbia gain independence from Turkey. Bulgaria becomes semi-autonomous.
1877-1914	European powers colonize Africa.
1884	Reform Act in Britain gives the vote to all males over 21.
1890	Luxembourg becomes independent from Holland.
	Forth railway bridge, the first large steel construction, is completed.
1895	Marconi invents the wireless.
	Sigmund Freud publishes his first work on psychoanalysis.
	Röntgen discovers "x-rays".
1897	After rising against Turkey, Crete becomes united with Greece.
1898	Pierre and Marie Curie observe radioactivity.
1900	Entrances to Paris Métro designed in *Art Nouveau* style.
1905	Norway gains independence from Sweden.
	Albert Einstein proposes his Theory of Relativity.
1908	Austria-Hungary takes Bosnia and Hercegovina from Turkey.
1911	Italy and Turkey at war.
1912	First Balkan War. Bulgaria, Greece, Serbia and Montenegro unite and defeat Turkey.
1913	Second Balkan War. Turkey, Romania, Serbia and Montenegro unite and defeat Bulgaria.
1914	Murder of Archduke Francis Ferdinand triggers First World War.
1916	Tanks used for first time at Battle of the Somme.
1917	Russian Revolution.

1918 Mar. Russia is defeated and makes peace with Germany.

1918 Nov. Germany signs an armistice with the Allies.

1919 Finland, Latvia, Lithuania, Estonia, Poland, Czechoslovakia, Yugoslavia, Austria and Hungary all become independent nations.

Britain gives vote to women over 30.

Mussolini establishes fascist movement in Italy.

Modernist school of architecture known as the Bauhaus founded in Germany.

1920 Ireland, except for Ulster in the north, becomes the Irish Free State (or Eire).

1922-1930s The Great Depression. Nearly every country in the world is hit by a deep economic crisis.

1922 Mussolini forms a fascist government in Italy.

1924 Lenin dies and is replaced by Stalin.

1928 Alexander Fleming discovers penicillin.

1933 Adolf Hitler, leader of the Nazis, becomes chancellor of Germany.

1936-39 The Spanish Civil War is fought between Spanish Nationalists, led by the fascist General Franco, and the mainly communist Republicans.

1939-75 Franco is dictator of Spain

1939 Sept. Hitler invades Poland.

1939-45 Second World War.

1943 Italy surrenders to the Allies.

1945 May Germany surrenders and is split into French, British, US and Russian occupation zones.

1945 Aug. USA drops atomic bombs on Japanese cities of Hiroshima and Nagasaki.

1945 Sept. Japan surrenders.

1946 USA announces Marshall Plan, an aid package for Europe.

1947 India is granted independence from Britain

1948 Communists seize power in Czechoslovakia, Hungary, Romania, Bulgaria and Poland.

1949 Dutch recognize the independence of Indonesia.

West and East Germany established as separate states.

Western powers form the North Atlantic Treaty Organization (NATO).

1953 Two scientists, Crick and Watson, work out the structure of the DNA molecule.

1954 France forced to leave colonies in Indo-China.

1955 USSR and Soviet bloc countries sign Warsaw Pact.

1956 Anti-communist uprising in Hungary crushed by USSR.

1957 Treaty of Rome, signed by Belgium, Italy, France, Germany, Luxembourg and the Netherlands, sets up the EEC.

USSR launches the first space satellite, *Sputnik I.*

Gold Coast (Ghana) becomes first of many black African countries to throw off colonial rule and win independence.

1960 Cyprus wins independence

1961 Yuri Gagarin (USSR) makes first manned spaceflight.

1961 Berlin Wall is built to prevent East Germans from fleeing to the West.

1968 Student unrest and strikes across Europe.

Clashes between Protestants and Catholics in Northern Ireland.

A liberal movement in Czechoslovakia is crushed by USSR.

1973 Denmark, Eire and United Kingdom join the EEC.

The innovative Spanish artist, Pablo Piccasso, dies aged 92.

1977 Centre Pompidou in Paris is completed.

1981 Greece joins the EEC.

1982 Argentina invades British Falkland Islands. Britain sends a naval taskforce and retakes islands.

1985 Mikhail Gorbachev becomes leader of the USSR.

1985 Nov. Ronald Reagan (US president) and Gorbachev meet for first time in Geneva.

1986 Spain and Portugal join the EEC.

1988 Reagan and Gorbachev sign an arms reductions treaty.

1989 Polish Solidarity movement legalized after an eight year ban.

1989 Sept. Hungary opens border to East German refugees.

1989 Nov. Berlin Wall is knocked down.

Communist leadership resigns in Czechoslovakia.

1989 Dec. Civil war in Romania.

1989-91 Popular demands for reform and democracy in Albania lead to unrest.

1990 Dec. Lech Walesa becomes president of Poland.

1991 Soviet troops begin a military crackdown in the Baltic States. President Gorbachev denies ordering the use of force.

President of Albania strengthens his powers to stop unrest. Many refugees flee to Greece and Italy.

Slovenia and Croatia declare themselves independent from Yugoslavia.

Yugoslavian president (a Serb) sends troops to Croatia and encourages Serbs in Croatia to fight against Croatians.

Coup by anti-reformists in USSR is defeated.

Latvia, Lithuania and Estonia become independent.

1991 Dec. Soviet Union officially ceases to exist. Many former Soviet republics become officially independent.

1992 Jan. A ceasefire agreement is signed between Croatia and Serbia (the largest and most powerful state in Yugoslavia), but sporadic fighting continues.

1992 Mar. Bosnia and Hercegovina declares itself independent from Yugoslavia after a vote boycotted by Bosnian Serbs.

Civil war breaks out in Bosnia and Hercegovina, mainly between Bosnian Serbs and Muslims. Bosnian Serbs are supported by Serbia.

1992 Maastricht Treaty drawn up.

Czechoslovakia divides into the Czech Republic and Slovakia.

1993 Civil war in Bosnia and Hercegovina continues.

GLOSSARY

Abdicate
To give up a throne or a position of power.

Absolute monarchy
A form of government in which the monarch (king or queen) has total control.

Alliance
A formal agreement, often military, between two or more countries.

Aristocracy
A privileged class of people, usually large landowners.

Armistice
An agreement between opposing armies to halt hostilities in order that peace talks may be held.

Assembly
A number of people who gather together for a formal meeting, often as part of government.

Authoritarian rule
Strict government by a small group of people with wide powers.

Autocracy
Government by one individual with unrestricted powers.

Blockade
The destruction by one nation of another nation's lines of communication and transport.

Bolshevik
Originally a Russian communist supporter of Lenin, who wanted immediate revolution. Today it is often used in a more general sense to describe any communist.

Capitalism
An economic system where the means of production (industries, factories and businesses) are owned by relatively few people, who provide the investment and take a large share of the profits.

Charter
A formal document issued by a ruler or government, granting certain rights or liberties, such as self-rule.

Christendom
Term used in the Middle Ages to refer to all the peoples, or nations, who belonged to the Christian Church.

Christianity
A religion based on the life and teachings of Jesus Christ.

Civilization
A highly developed society with its own political and legal systems, its own art and architecture and often a form of writing.

Civil War
War between parties or factions within the same nation.

Class
A collection of people sharing a similar social, economic and cultural position.

Classical Age
A period in Ancient Greek history when many great developments occurred in art, architecture, politics and economics.

Classical
Of Classical Greek or Roman origin or style.

Clergy
Men and women who are committed to a religious life within the Christian Church (priests, monks and nuns).

Collectivization
The organization by the state of the ownership of the means of production into groups or collectives.

Colony
A country or an area of land held and ruled by another country, sometimes against the wishes of the inhabitants.

Communism
An ideology mainly based on the ideas of Karl Marx. It promotes a society without social classes or private ownership, in which the means of production (industries) are owned by the state.

Democracy
A system of government, originating in Ancient Greece, which involves rule by the people or by their elected representatives.

Deportation
The act of transporting a person out of a country, usually against their will.

Dictatorship
A non-royal autocratic rule, in which a dictator imposes his position by force.

Dissenter
Someone who disagrees with an established system of beliefs. Particularly one who refuses to belong to the established church of a nation.

Economy
The system of distribution, buying and selling of goods and services in a country.

Emigration
Leaving one country to settle in another.

Enlightenment
An 18th century movement which stressed the importance of reason.

Excommunicate
To expel a person from the Christian Church.

Exile
An enforced absence from one's country.

Fascism
A nationalist ideology developed by the Italian politician, Benito Mussolini. A form of government which allows no rival parties and which controls the lives of its citizens. Nazism is a form of fascism.

Federation
A type of government in which power is shared between a central parliament and several regional governments.

Feudalism
A social and economic system that developed in western Europe in the 8th and 9th centuries. People were protected by local lords. In return, they served under them in war or worked on their land.

Glasnost
The policy of openness and freedom, developed in the USSR under the leadership of Mikhail Gorbachev.

Government
The act of ruling, or the group of people who rule a country.

Guilds
Medieval organizations of workers with the same craft or profession, formed to maintain craft standards, to set wages and prices and to protect workers.

Humanism
A belief that people can advance themselves by their own efforts without, for example, the help of a religion.

Industrialization
The development of a country's industries and factories, so that its economic existence is no longer solely based on farming.

Inflation
A rise in the price of most goods and commodities.

Islam
The religion of Muslims, based on the life and teachings of the prophet Mohammed.

Judaism
The religion of the Jews, people descended from ancient tribes called the Israelites. Its central idea is the belief in one God who created everything.

Lay
Relating to people who do not belong to the clergy.

Liberal
Having social and political views that emphasize progress and reform.

Media
All the different means and agencies (e.g. television and newspapers) for communicating information to the public.

Medieval
Relating to the Middle Ages, a period in European history dating from about 1000-1500.

Mercenaries
Soldiers who do not belong to the army of any particular nation, but who fight in wars in return for wages.

Moderate
A person who does not hold extreme political views.

Modernism
A term used to describe experimental methods used in different art forms (painting, architecture, writing, etc.) which began at the start of the 20th century.

Monarchy
A form of government in which power and authority are given to one person, such as a king, who usually inherits the position.

Nationalism
A sense of common identity based on a shared culture or language which binds a population together. It often produces the desire for independence from foreign rule. Taken to extreme levels, it can lead to aggression against other nations.

Papacy
The office or position of Pope.

Parliament
A meeting place for decision-making and law-giving, usually incorporating some sort of assembly.

Peasant
A member of a class who depends on agricultural labour to make a living. Someone at the bottom of the feudal system.

Perestroika
The policy of restructuring the economy in the USSR, begun by Mikhail Gorbachev.

Persecution
The act of maltreating people, usually because of race or religion.

Propaganda
The organized broadcasting of information in order to publicize the aims and achievements of a particular political group or a set of beliefs.

Protestant
A member of a Protestant (non-Catholic) Church.

Reformation
A reform movement in the Christian Church, started by Martin Luther's criticisms of the Catholic Church in the early 16th century. It led to the establishment of Protestant churches.

Renaissance
A period of intellectual and artistic development in 14th-15th century Europe, inspired by Greek and Roman civilization.

Republic
A state governed by the representatives of the people, without a king or queen.

Resistance
An illegal organization fighting for liberty in a country under enemy occupation.

Revolution
The overthrow of a regime or political system by those who are governed.

Royalist
A supporter of the monarchy.

Sacking
The plunder and destruction of a place by an army or a mob.

Self-government
The government of a country by its own people, rather than a foreign power.

Semi-autonomous
Describes a country which is still the possession of another state, but which has a large degree of self-government.

Socialism
An ideology that values equality of income and wealth, and believes in public (state) ownership of the means of production (industries).

Stalinism
The theory and form of communist government associated with Stalin, characterized by dictatorship and brutal repression of opponents.

Terrorism
The use of terror, for instance bomb attacks and assassinations, as a means of political persuasion.

Trade unions
Associations of workers formed to improve working conditions and pay and to state grievances to employers.

Tribute
Payment made by one nation or people to another more dominant nation or people.

INDEX

The publishers are grateful to the following organizations for permission to reproduce their material or to use it as artist's reference:

The J. Allan Cash Photolibrary, 6 (Rhine Valley)
Norwegian Tourist Board, London, 6 (Fjord)
The Mansell Collection, 20 (Artist's reference for Venice)
Vatican Museums and Galleries, Rome; Bridgeman Art Library, London, 22 (Raphael's The School of Athens)
Royal Collection, Windsor, 22 (Artist's reference for Leonardo da Vinci's drawings)
Michael Holford©, 24
Giraudon; Bridgeman Art Library, London, 27
Imperial War Museum, London, 30
Hulton Deutsch Collection, London, 31
Novosti, London, 32 (Karl Marx and The Storming of the Winter Palace)
Altgubyoyenkomat Politprosvet Press, Barnaul, 32 (Soviet poster)
Novosti, London, 33
Ullstein Bildereinst, Berlin, 34
Weimar Archive, Great Britain, 35

Novosti, London, 37
Ullstein Bilderienst, Berlin, 39 (East German border guard)
Sovietsky Khudozhnik, Moscow, 39 (Soviet poster)
Novosti, London, 44 (Mikhail Gorbachev and Ronald Reagan)
Hulton Deutsch Collection, London, 44 (Lech Walesa)
Popperfoto, 45
British Library, London; Bridgeman Art Library, London, 46, Izobrazitelnoye Iskusstvo, Moscow, 47

First published in 1993 by Usborne Publishing Ltd, Usborne House, 83-85 Saffron Hill, London EC1N 8RT, England.
Copyright © 1993 Usborne Publishing Ltd. The name Usborne and the device ⯑ are Trade Marks of Usborne Publishing Ltd. All rights reserved. No part of this publication may be reproduced, stored in a retrieval system or transmitted in any form or by any means, electronic, mechanical, photocopying, recording or otherwise, without the prior permission of the publisher. UE First published in America March 1994.
Printed in Great Britain.